WHAT DID I SAY?

KIMBERLY D GRAHAM

WHAT DID I SAY?

Kimberly D Graham

XULON PRESS

© 2019 by Kimberly D. Graham

What Did I Say?
by Kimberly D. Graham

Printed in the United States of America.

ISBN-13:978-1-54565-670-9

All rights reserved solely by the author. The author guarantees all contents are original and do not infringe upon the legal rights of any other person or work. No part of this book may be reproduced in any form without the permission of the author. The views expressed in this book are not necessarily those of the publisher.

Unless otherwise indicated, Scripture quotations taken from the King James Version (KJV) – *public domain.*

Scripture quotations taken from the Holy Bible, New Living Translation (NLT). Copyright ©1996, 2004, 2007 by Tyndale House Foundation. Used by permission of Tyndale House Publishers, Inc.

Scripture quotations taken from the Holy Bible, New International Version (NIV). Copyright © 1973, 1978, 1984, 2011 by Biblica, Inc.™. Used by permission. All rights reserved.

www.xulonpress.com

ACKNOWLEDGEMENTS

Thank You Lord, for blessing me with gifts and abilities to help others in their quest to being better people.

I am so grateful for my family and friends who continuously encourage me to use my God given gifts to increase the Kingdom of God. No one believes in me like my brother Marvell Mitchell; he is probably somewhere right now telling someone about me. I love you man!

Special thanks to my mother whose words are sweet, funny and comforting. I always know where to go when I need unconditional love.

An extra special Thank you to Deborah Dupree a.k.a. Queen who took time and energy to help edit my book. Oh, my goodness, the fun we had, the memories we created, the friendship and lasting bond we formed. I was in need and God loved me enough to cause me to be in the place to hear you talk about the love you have for things being correct. Thank you for saying yes to God by saying yes to me, this book would not be as awesome as it is without your creativity, I love you!

I thank my children Javon and Alexis for cheering me on, you two are the reason I strive to be my best. Jerry, my loving husband, I thank God for blessing me with you. My journey is so much more exciting because I get to do it with you. I love you forever, Kim, your wife for life!

TABLE OF CONTENTS

Preface xi
Introduction: *What Did I Say?* xv
Day 1: Doubt 1
Day 2: Fear 11
Day 3: Offense 25
Day 4: Disappointment 33
Day 5: Complaining 43
Day 6: Worry 53
Day 7: Regret 61
Day 8: Trust 77
Day 9: Fight Back 89
Day 10: Forgive and Forget 101
Day 11: I Want to Change 115
Day 12: In My Way 129
Day 13: Empower Yourself 139

Day 14: Attention 149

Day 15: Celebrate 163

Day 16: Let God Arise 173

Day 17: Can My Dream Still Manifest? 185

Day 18: Starting Over 195

Day 19: No More Shrinking 209

Day 20: When You Know Better, Do Better! 221

Day 21: The Struggle Within 233

Day 22: Remember 243

Day 23: Don't Let Your Mind Kill You 257

Day 24: Created to. 273

Day 25: Next in Line 281

Day 26: Be Healed 291

Day 27: The Blood of Jesus! 301

Day 28: Create Your Own Legacy 305

Day 29: If You Just Believe 315

Day 30: Assurance 327

Preface

I prayed years ago inquiring of my God-given gifts and how they should be used to be a blessing to others as well as me. At the time of my inquiry, I was teaching a Bible study to school age children as well as attending the university. While in school, I recall completing an essay and asking a stranger in the computer lab to read it over for me.

The first thing she asked was, "What's the name of this book?"

I told her it wasn't a book, it was bits and pieces of my life. I then asked, "If it was a book, would you read it?"

Without hesitation, she said, "Yes!"

That was my first inkling that my writing was pretty good. The second one came from a college professor who taught an online course that I completed. I had to write essays for the class. The compliments the teacher gave me regarding my writing just blew me away and made me say to myself, *Maybe I really am good at this.*

The last confirmation came when I prayed. We were in church and our pastor at the time was praying for people who knew what their gifts were and would agree they would be successful using them. I stayed in the back because I had no clue.

The next day, a friend left a message on my voicemail saying, "Kim, I know we have never spoken of this, but God told me to tell you that you are a writer."

At that point, without a doubt I knew that was my gift. The moment I said yes to God regarding using my gift, He gave me the first three book titles and the order to write them. I say this to share I knew what this title would be years ago, however, I didn't know all I would have to encounter and endure to write it.

This has been quite a journey and what I know for sure is it wasn't for nothing. Everyone is on a journey and we all need each other at some point in time to help us along the way. I love God, I love Jesus, and I love Holy Spirit. I love being a Christian. I share that to say, no one could have ever told me that I would have moments of doubt and unbelief.

Preface

Moments when I would experience extreme fear and do things that caused shame.

From the moment I read in the Bible about the power of the tongue, I have been saying, "Speak life." Who knew there would be times when I would choose to speak the opposite? I would say crazy things and then would say to myself, *What did you just say? You know better.*

I had serious trust issues and from time to time found it hard to fully obey. No one could have ever told me, my journey would have consisted of such, but it wasn't all bad. There were good, great, and amazing moments, in fact, more of them than bad and for that I am thankful. When God gave me the name of the books before the first one was ever written, I was oblivious to a lot of things. Since then, my conversations with Him have evolved.

"What Did I Say?" is a book full of reminders of how much our heavenly Father loves us. Life can be challenging sometimes and who better to talk to about our life than God. We can talk to Him about anything, and we should, because He has the answer to everything.

So, as you read and go through this 30-Day Devotional, my hope is you will receive clarity about some things and become willing to let go of what has been holding you back from living life authentically. At some point, it may be a bit challenging to be open and honest but believe me it will be freeing. After reading this book, you will be glad you had these needed conversations.

Enjoying partaking in conversations with our loving heavenly Father, who wants nothing but the best for His children.

Introduction

WHAT DID I SAY?

Every time you talk to Me, I hear you. Every time you ask Me a question, I answer you. The problem is not that I am not speaking, the problem is you are not listening; and when you do, you do not adhere to My words.

What did I say?

You can talk to Me about everything. Nothing is too deep or too personal. I have the answers to your questions; I am the solution. What do you think I mean when you read Proverbs 3:6, "In all thy ways acknowledge him, and he shall direct thy paths"? I AM not, nor have I ever been the problem. How do you think I feel when you pray, I answer, then you say after you have ignored my instructions,

"Something told me to do. . .."? The Holy Spirit is not a something! The Holy Spirit is a person; read your Bible, gain knowledge and confidence.

I did not create you to be like anyone else; you are unique. Stop trying to fit in. You were created to stand out. I am really frustrated by your lack of trust and belief in Me.

Have I not proven Myself to you?

Think about that question for a moment. I have always been there, and the Holy Spirit has always brought that to your remembrance. You have not lacked any good thing and I am bold enough to make that statement. You might say, "But Father there was that time when I didn't have what I needed." My response is, "I supplied your need and you did not use it for its purpose." Do we need to go back and forth like this because I can supply the proof? It is time for you to grow up and start taking responsibility for your own decisions and actions. I am here for you always. Jesus has done His part and Holy Spirit is on assignment.

Introduction

What will you do? When will you start doing it?

It is time you become a doer of My Word, not just a hearer (James 1:22). The thoughts I have toward you are great, so My expectation of you is great.

What will you do with the information I have given you?

You have sixty-six books on your nightstand and scriptures at your fingertips.

Why are you still the same?
Who are you trying to fool?
What did I say?

My Word should be hidden in your heart, so you will not sin against Me, (Psalm 119:11) and end up staying the same. I AM disappointed in what I see in you. I am not mad; the love I have for you will not allow it. I will always love you! I am being a little tough on you right now, but you can handle it. You know my correction is out of love (Proverbs 3:12).

Say ouch if you need to, get mad, and even cry, but once you are finished, smile.

Smile because I care, smile because you are here, smile because I love you, and smile because I am near. You have a reason to praise Me! Take a deep breath; you have a reason to serve Me. Look where you are today; you have a reason to follow Me. Let us make the rest of your life the best of your life! It is not too late.

Do not fret, remember Who you are working with and remember what I have said. A thousand years is as a day to Me (2 Peter 3:8), so you are alright. You do not have to play catch up, so do not rush; pace yourself, get in the game, and run your race. Life does not have to happen to you, it can happen for you if you learn how to live it.

Will you listen to Me from this moment on?
Will you trust your intuition and every other protective instinct I have given you?
Will you begin to act like you know that I love you and that I have your back?
Will you work on your relationship with Me?
Will you continue to walk with confidence?

Introduction

Your life is not meant to be hard, so stop making it hard. Stop blending in and stop allowing fear to shut you up. I gave you a mouth for a reason, use it to speak life and get yourself out of the situation you put yourself in. I love you and now it is time to show Me that you love Me, too.

Day 1
Doubt

"Doubt is to waver or fluctuate in opinion; to hesitate; to be in suspense; to be in uncertainty, to be undetermined."

(KJV *Dictionary*)

There were people in the Bible and those we know about in history who were full of faith, yet experienced moments of doubt. One man exclaimed in Mark 9:24, "I believe, help my unbelief." So, if you have doubted in life, you are not alone.

God is good! Every time you talk to Him, He listens. He cares for you and has an answer for every question you ask and a statement for every thought you ponder. As you continue to read, you will find a conversation I had with God regarding my doubt. I pray that as you read, you will be moved and learn more about your doubts.

Heavenly Father, I keep seeing myself in a grand place doing great things, however, currently, that is not the case. Should I believe these dreams and visions or disregard them and put them in the pile of things that made me smile for a while? At times I feel like I am being teased because I am nowhere near what I see. I believe in the dreams, I get excited about the dreams and I fully expect them to come true, however, there are times when I doubt.

Do you really want to know what's going on?

The problem you are experiencing is common with My children. You, just like a lot of the others, are not working toward fulfilling your purpose. As your Heavenly Father, I give you dreams and show you visions so that you will get happy and work toward accomplishing them. Instead, you stop and stare and wonder if your dream is even possible. You worry about "how" this will happen, instead of simply believing. Remember, nothing is impossible for Me (Mark 10:27).

Your dreams can be your reality.

Stop starting and stopping. You will never see what I see in you if you keep stopping. You said earlier the dreams you see make you smile, so why not work to make them your reality?

The feelings you have that come along with your doubts are self-inflicted. You know enough about Me to make things happen for yourself, but you choose to sit and stare.

Snap out of it! Stop walking around like the walking dead. You are not in the valley of dry bones (Ezekiel 37:1-14).

Start living. Blood is running warm through your veins for a reason. You have a purpose in this life.

Stop talking and start doing!

You cannot keep talking about your dream without doing something about it. Faith without works is dead (James 2:20) and dead weight is a heavy load to carry. Dead weight creates stagnation and stagnation creates procrastination. Procrastination creates lack of motivation which ignites complaining and breeds jealousy and envy.

Who told you it could not be done?

I created you with gifts and talents and gave you everything you would need to use them to become a great person. Doubt did not come from Me. It is something you picked up from listening to the wrong voices. Do not let people who do not believe in your gift stop you from believing in yourself. Do not be fooled. There is a real enemy that wants to keep you from the truth, but I want you to know the truth and be free (John 8:32).

Everything I created is good.

Everything I created is good and because you were made in My image, so are the things you create. Get started! Your time is too precious to waste. There is no more confirmation needed. You have got it all. Your job at this moment is to believe what I have said and believe in yourself.

Dare to be different! Dare to start living your dream. Dare to look fear in the eye and walk in the truth. Dare to say "yes" to My will and My way of life for you. Dare to say "yes" to endless possibilities.

What did I say?

Father, I heard You say I am not consistently working as I should and what I am doing is stopping and staring. You said a lot of what I am going through is self-inflicted. I am alive and there is no part of me in the valley of dry bones, so I should stop procrastinating and live. I need to stop listening to the wrong voices and start listening to what You say.

Thoughts for you, the Reader...

Now it's your turn. Are you ready to acknowledge your doubts?

What is your experience with doubt?

_____

_____

_____

_____

What are your dreams?

_____

_____

_____

_____

What barriers/negative voices are keeping you from working toward your dreams?

_____

_____

_____

_____

Doubt

What self-inflicted or questionable feelings have they caused?

Review the scriptures given for this day and record what God reveals to you.

Mark 9:24

Mark 10:27

Ezekiel 37:1-14

James 2:20

John 8:32

When you consider your doubts, what do you hear God say?

Today's Prayer: *Thank You, Lord, for blessing me to be a part of this day. Thank You for teaching me the workings of doubt. I will no longer allow doubt to keep me from fulfilling the purpose and calling You have for my life. Thank You for the dreams and for giving me all I need to pursue them. Lord, I am listening.*

Today's Affirmations

(Say Aloud)

I am Confident.

I am a Believer.

I am Capable of. . .(fill in the blank)

Write Your Vision

I decree and declare from this moment forward I will _____

_____

_____

_____

_____

_____

_____

_____

_____

_____

_____

Day 2
Fear

"Fear is a painful emotion or passion excited by an expectation of evil, or the apprehension of impending danger."

(KJV *Dictionary*)

God is love! God loves us so much that He made it possible for us to come to Him and come boldly before His throne of grace. A healthy relationship with God the Father, a reverence for His sovereignty, and knowledge of His love for us is what we need to live the abundant life Jesus came to give us. As humans, we all have experienced some form of fear. However, the spirit of fear is not of God. Remember, God is love, and perfect love casts out all fear (1 John 4:18).

I must admit I have certain fears, but the fear of failure is probably at the top of my list. I always want to be the best I can be in everything. When I fall short of my own expectations, it's the hardest pill to swallow. When I don't meet my goals, I then experience fear that what God has promised me will not manifest. That's one type of fear, but another type I have experienced was worse.

There was a season in my life when I truly had the spirit of fear on me. It was unshakable for a very long time. During the day, from time to time fearful thoughts plagued my mind. However, at night it was worse. It was as if the enemy and his imps waited until I rested my head and closed my eyes to really attack my mind with thoughts filled with fear. I spent many nights staying awake as long as I could to avoid the fight in my sleep that was inevitable. It was truly one of the worse seasons in my life.

As I talked to the Lord about my experiences regarding fear, He spoke to me and reminded me of the purpose of fear, the power attached to fear, and what His Word says about fear. As you continue to read, you will see how I embraced God's response to my fear. I had to learn to conquer my fear and believe God. Now let God offer some answers for yours.

Do Not Fear

Fear comes to move you out of position. I [God the Father] created you with no fear. To function authentically, you must operate courageously. I hear people say, "Scared money don't make money," and I say, "Scared people don't have money to make." If you are scared, pray. Talk to Me and tell Me all about what has you so afraid, so I can tell you what you need. You know some things in part, but I know **all** things. I can help you if you talk to Me. I want to help you.

Fear is not from Me. It is a hindrance to your preparation. Love cancels fear, and I love you! When I give you an assignment, I equip you for it, so there is nothing to fear. To be nervous is natural, but to be fearful is not your natural (original) state of being. I understand fear entered your life, but it does not have to stay there. Remember, you are made in My image and I am not afraid of anything.

Remember the enemy's mission statement
and the mission of fear.

Satan is the father of lies and he tells them all the time. In fact, the more you believe his lies, the more he tells them to you and the more he tells, the more fearful you become. Fear messes things up. How many times have you acted out of fear and your situation went from bad to worse? How many times did you believe lies over the truth? Lies were being told and your intuition told you they were lies, but because you loved the one telling them, you ignored the truth and continued to be bound. Be aware of wolves in sheep's clothing (Matthew 7:15); misery loves company.

Am I telling you this to insight more fear? No! Remember, fear did not come from Me. I am telling you this because you need to know. I am telling you this because I love you!

Satan's plan never changes, it is to steal, kill, and destroy (John 10:10). Fear is a hidden component in the enemy's mission. When you are fearful, your peace is stolen, your confidence is nonexistent, and your goals are destroyed.

Be alert and pay attention.

Fear is **F**alse **E**vidence **A**ppearing **R**eal. Think about that for a moment. Just because something appears a certain way does not mean it is that way. Satan is as a roaring lion (1 Peter 5:8), he is not the Lion of Judah. In fact, he is a toothless lion. He just makes noise to startle you and get you responding to the noise in a way that strengthens him in your life. Do not be fooled!

There are no new tricks.

There is nothing new under the sun (Ecclesiastes 1:9) and there is an answer for everything. Do not allow the noise the enemy stirs up cause you to fear; instead, let it strengthen your faith because you know Me and know that I love you! You know that I would not allow anything to hurt you, so if there is noise in your life right now, silence it with your faith and My Word.

See yourself higher!

Picture the most fearless person you know or have heard of, past or present. Now, imagine yourself being as fearless. What you imagine, I have seen in you. It took faith. Although fear tried to squeeze through the cracks, you conquered it.

There came a time when you no longer cared about the whispers and the negative suggestions. Your curiosity about your dreams and everything I told you finally got the best of you and you went for it. You finally saw yourself as worthy to have what you want and you got it. So many others received what they wanted also because they were watching you. Your actions spoke louder than your words, and a revolution got started. People began looking at themselves differently and speaking about things that mattered and eventually, they produced great things. The things that were produced healed sicknesses in communities and before long, people began to thrive.

When you walk in courage, it gives others the confidence to do the same. It is important to conquer the spirit of fear. Remember, fear comes to move you out of position, not the position you see right now, but the position I saw back then.

What did I say?

Father, what I heard You tell me is that fear comes to move me out of position by hindering all I prepare to do. You said fear did not come from You and that I need to stop listening to the lies being told to me by the devil. You said fear is false evidence that appears real, but love cancels it all. You told me to walk in confidence, and when I do, it will give others the confidence to do the same.

Thoughts for you, the Reader...

It's your turn...

What is/are your fear(s)?

_____
_____
_____
_____

How has fear moved you from a place of security and hindered you from progress?

_____
_____
_____
_____

How has your response to fear caused a situation to move from bad to worse?

_____
_____
_____
_____

Fear

How do you see faith helping you overcome your fear(s)?

___

Review the scriptures given for this day and record what God reveals to you.

1 John 4:18

___

Matthew 7:15

___

John 10:10

___

1 Peter 5:8

_____

_____

_____

_____

Ecclesiastes 1:9

_____

_____

_____

_____

Genesis 26:24

_____

_____

_____

_____

When you consider your fear(s), what do you hear God say?

_____

_____

_____

_____

Today's Prayer: *Thank You, God, for showing me the dangers of the spirit of fear. I release fear from my life right now in Jesus' name. I will no longer allow fear to bind me and keep me from fulfilling the purpose and calling You have for my life. Thank You for the dreams and for giving me all I need to pursue them. Please know that I am listening and I will work to do what You say.*

Today's Affirmation

(Say Aloud)

I am Fearless.

I am Worthy.

I am Capable of. . .(fill in the blank)

Write Your Vision

I decree and declare from this moment forward I will _____

_____
_____
_____
_____
_____
_____
_____
_____
_____
_____
_____

Day 3
Offense

"Offend is to displease; to make angry; to wrong."

(KJV *Dictionary*)

God is Smart! God is the Master Creator, so He knows the inner workings of everything. There is nothing created for which God is not aware; no hidden agendas, no secret components, He knows everything. He knows why it is good to do certain things and He knows why it is not. God will never tell us to do something wrong and allowing offense to be a part of our character is not right.

When I think back, there were times when I allowed myself to be easily offended. It seemed like any little thing would set me off and have me pouting and holding grudges. I have learned that offense is a weapon used by the enemy to stop me from being my best. When I carried offense with me, I didn't try as hard or do as much because I had the negative situation on my mind and at times in my heart. As I talked to God about why I was so easily offended, His response can be found in the thread below.

Do not be easily offended.

One of the greatest problems I see and have seen for a while is offense, God impressed upon me. People offend. At times, it is deliberate and other times it is not, but regardless of the motive, you must work on your response to it. I do not want you to take offense personally. Look at the offender as one who does not know better or truly does not know you.

Offense is a killer. It is a known cause of relationship problems as well as the destruction of them. No one wins when offense is present. Offense is something to which one should not react negatively, instead see it as an opportunity to grow. It is a way of being enlightened about an individual or situation.

Do you know the benefits of being a child of God?

I need to get you to a place of knowing that you win in every situation. The only way I can do that is to continuously remind you of who you are, My child. You are a winner. All things work together for your good (Romans 8:28). Some benefits to name a few are: You have complete access to Me, (I am all yours), you can ask anything of Me in My Son's name (Jesus is the way), and through repentance, your sins are forgiven (just ask).

Perspective is everything.

Change the way you see things and their meaning will change. Knowing this truth takes away the offense and puts purpose in its place. Purpose makes everything alright because purpose has meaning. Purpose makes offense tolerable. Just as antibiotics help heal infections, offense and your response to it can help build character. There is absolutely nothing you can do to stop offense from occurring. Your role is to choose not to be offended by the offenses. This will take time and practice as you implement what you learn from My Word along the way.

Protect your gift, your dreams, and yourself.

Never allow anything or anyone to steal your joy. The joy you have comes from Me. It is a gift, one of the many symbols of My love for you. Joy is powerful! It can brighten the darkest room, dry the wettest eye, and calm your most raging sea. When you allow joy to overflow from you, it will please your best friend and confuse your biggest foe.

I made you powerful and equipped you with everything you will need to live a powerfully blessed life; so, live it! You matter to Me and your dreams matter to the world, so shake off the offenses. What someone said or did to you does not compare to what I want to do for you. I love you. If you can truly let go of what no longer matters, you will soon see that there are no limits to what you can have, and all your impossibilities will be possible. Offenses kill; do not be their next victim.

What did I say?

Wow, Lord, You said a lot. I didn't realize what I was doing to myself by holding on to offenses. You said people offend, sometimes on purpose and other times accidentally, but I am not to allow offense into my life. Offense has the power to kill relationships. Everything happens for a reason and when offense reveals itself, I need to look at what it came to show me about myself and not be provoked. There are dangerous traps in life and carrying offense is a liability.

Offense

Thoughts for you, the Reader...

If you are carrying offense, now is a good time to let it go.

What has offended you?

_____
_____
_____

How did it offend you?

_____
_____
_____

When you think about the person(s) who caused the offense(s), what were the red flags that you ignored?

_____
_____
_____
_____

Review the scripture given for this day and record what God reveals to you.

Romans 8:28

_____
_____
_____
_____

When you consider being offended or carrying offense, what do you hear God say?

_____
_____
_____
_____

Today's Prayer: *Thank You, Lord, for teaching me the dangers of offense. I now know that offense is a weapon used to steal, kill, and destroy those You love. I no longer allow it to be a part of my life. I will seek Your counsel and ask for help when confronted. I forgive each offense and every offender, in Jesus' name. Thank You for showing me how to recognize the traps and stay clear of them. I am listening to what You say and I will do what You tell me to do. I love myself enough to do this work and I love You for Your guidance and direction in this walk.*

Today's Affirmations

(Say Aloud)

I am Content

I am Good Natured

I am Capable of. . .(fill in the blank)

Write Your Vision

I decree and declare from this moment forward I will _____

_____

_____

_____

_____

_____

_____

_____

_____

_____

_____

_____

Day 4
Disappointment

"Disappoint: to fail or meet the expectation or hope of."
(Merriam-Webster Dictionary)

God is caring! He loves us so much that He has given us a Comforter in the person of the Holy Spirit whom not only comforts, He leads, guides, and does so much more because of love. When disappointment shows up, just know you are never alone. God cares and will be with you.

I have experienced a lot of disappointment, some I understood and some I did not. In fact, there were times when God spoke to me about my perspective concerning my situations and my disappointment immediately changed. In the dialogue on disappointment that follows, may you find a connection and receive revelation.

Your thoughts and ways are not like Mine.

{Sigh}, I thought it was going to work out. I was invested in it and emotionally tied to it, but it didn't. I felt betrayed in the process and angry afterward; I was disappointed. "What did I miss and why did I miss it?" My feelings were hurt and my heart was slightly bruised, all because it didn't work.

Who says it did not work?

It did work, however, not the way you expected, but exactly the way it should have. You are disappointed because you ignored the signs that led to the outcome. Be very clear of why you are hurting and put blame where it belongs. I know it can be hard to admit when you are wrong, but admitting can be freeing. When you take responsibility for your actions, people and situations have no power to disappoint you.

Everyone has experienced hurt.

I understand that seeds were planted and things were done to you or things happened that affected you. I want you to know, you can be healed. You are still here for a reason and that reason is not to live in the past. People who are hurt tend to hurt others. Some of them inflict pain on purpose and others do it accidentally, however, I do understand the hurt. Pain is inevitable; go through it with confidence and once it passes, the promise of joy will come and bring clarity and the right perspective regarding it.

Get to the good part.

Closed doors are not bad, so do not curse them; they are full of protection and opportunity. I love you! Do you think I would close a door if it was good for you? Stop getting caught up on how pretty the door is or how lucrative you think going through the door will be and start acknowledging Me, so I can lead you to the right door (Proverbs 3:6). I am here for you!

You would be in awe if only you believed all things are possible!

Disappointment can be a thing of the past for you if you would get in My presence and acknowledge Me in all your ways. I know it sounds crazy and a bit impossible, but in Me all things are possible (Matthew 19:26). You can live the life you were born to live if you would live it with Me. Sure, you may be doing okay, but okay compared to great is a big difference. Talk to Me and speak from your heart about what you really want.

What do you hear Me saying?

Father, what I hear You saying is my life can be so much better if I would truly surrender my ways of doing things and allow You to teach me Your ways. I need to take responsibility for my actions and be honest with myself. Some of my disappointments were self-inflicted because there were red flags and warning signs that I ignored. From this moment forward, I choose to listen and fully submit to the leading and guidance of the Holy Spirit.

Disappointment

Thoughts for you, the Reader...

Have you had moments of disappointment and are you ready to accept responsibility? If so, consider the following questions:

What do you consider a major disappointment in your life?

_____
_____
_____
_____

What were the causes?

_____
_____
_____
_____

What were your expectations?

_____
_____
_____
_____

What were the red flags and warning signs that you ignored?

When the chance comes for you to do it again, what will you do differently?

Review the scriptures given for this day and record what God reveals to you.

Proverbs 3:6

Matthew 19:26

Disappointment

When you consider disappointment, what do you hear God say?

_____

_____

_____

_____

Today's Prayer: *Lord, I thank You for the love You have for me. I will not doubt Your love nor Your instructions. I have been disappointed for the wrong reasons, and now that I know better, I will do better. I will not continue to make excuses, instead, I will make progress. I will become who You created me to be by fulfilling the purpose and calling You have for my life. Lord, I am listening.*

Today's Affirmations
(Say Aloud)

I am Encouraged.

I am Reasonable

I am Capable of. . .(fill in the blank)

Write Your Vision

I decree and declare from this moment forward I will _____

_____
_____
_____
_____
_____
_____
_____
_____
_____
_____
_____

Day 5
Complaining

"To complain is to utter expressions of grief; to lament."
(KJV Dictionary)

God is patient. God always listens to His children, but as it says in the Bible (Exodus and Numbers), there are times when the murmuring and complaining becomes annoying and yields negative outcomes.

Unfortunately, I have had my share of complaining. It isn't a great look and the sound of it is worse. I have learned that complaining about a problem without a solution for the problem is unnecessary noise to the atmosphere. I have since minimized my desire to complain (thank God). The following conversation was full of me complaining and venting to God. His response was a blessing to me. Read on and find your blessing.

Comparing yourself with another is a trap.

Why does it seem like it is hard for me to get ahead? I look around and it seems like some things are a breeze for so many people, however, it is such a challenge for me. I know I have great ideas and good intentions, but when it comes to implementing them, I never know how to do them or I lack the help needed. It doesn't seem fair. All I seem to do is spectate and I know You created me to do more. What is my problem? It's obviously me.

Do you listen to yourself speak?

Are you finished complaining about how unfair your life seems? You sound like the man at the pool of Bethesda (John 5:1-9) full of excuses. He knew he wanted to be well, but he was full of excuses. When Jesus asked him if he wanted to be well he made, yet another excuse. Stop making excuses! Your life is not bad. I could give it to another and not only would they be grateful, they would find ways to prosper with it. You know what your problem is? You do not listen.

Do not argue, do not complain, just listen.

You do not listen to Me, thus, the reason for your uncertainties regarding your life and the complaints I hear. I have not left you nor are My ears clogged to your cries. Your confusion stems from being double-minded (James 1:8). I have not forgotten about you, nor am I withholding your dreams; I am waiting on you. Do you know what you really want? A lot of your complaints come from you not knowing what you want. When your heart is honest and you are true to yourself, manifestation will come.

Be a doer of My Word.

Do not merely listen to My Word, be a doer of it. Devise a plan for what you desire, write your vision, and make it plain (Habakkuk 2:2). Get yourself ready, set your mind on your vision, and go for it! You can do this! Stop giving your attention to what is outside of you and embrace what is within. Do you not know you have the greater one on the inside (1 John 4:4), and He will always cause you to be triumphant? Do not be one who complains about your life, especially when you do nothing to enhance it.

Turn the page.

This is your season to make the best of it and get the most out of it. Do not look back and do not sabotage yourself by complaining. Learn to be grateful for everything, that includes the things you may never understand. Just be grateful and remember, your life is not bad. Get focused and move forward.

What did I say?

Lord, I heard You tell me that I am full of excuses regarding why I am where I am and that I should stop making them. I realize I should be grateful for the life You have given me. You said my double-mindedness has constructed a veil of confusion. I now reach deep within myself to begin the construction of my vision. . . my next great chapter.

Thoughts for you, the Reader...

Complaining is unproductive. It affects everyone.

How has complaining impacted your life?
_____
_____
_____
_____

What's your complaint?
_____
_____
_____
_____

Why do you think you are in your current predicament?
_____
_____
_____
_____

What will you do to overcome it?

___

Review the scriptures given for this day and record what God reveals to you.

Exodus 16

___

Numbers Chapters 11, 14, 16

___

John 5:1-9

___

Complaining

James 1:8

_____
_____
_____
_____

Habakkuk 2:2

_____
_____
_____
_____

1 John 4:4

_____
_____
_____
_____

When you consider the things you complain about, what do you hear God say?

_____
_____
_____
_____

Today's Prayer: *Lord, I thank You for showing me what I have been doing to myself, my dreams, and my purpose. I have allowed the why ME's to hinder the best of me from being displayed. I will no longer do that to myself. I accept what You allow to take place in me during this growth process. I am determined to fulfill my life's purpose and calling. Lord, I am here listening. When I truly think of Your goodness and mercy toward me, I have no reason to complain. I am blessed and I will do better in Jesus' name, Amen.*

Today's Affirmations

(Say Aloud)

I am Grateful

I am Hopeful

I am Capable of. . .(fill in the blank)

Write Your Vision

I decree and declare from this moment forward I will _____

_____
_____
_____
_____
_____
_____
_____
_____
_____
_____

Day 6
Worry

"Worry is to choke, to strangle."
(Merriam-Webster Dictionary)

God is peace. There is no good thing in worry. I once heard it said like this, "Worry is interest paid on a debt you may never owe." That statement came to me at a time when I allowed worry to get in me. I was able to conquer it for a season and later it came back with a vengeance.

In my conversation with God, He shared the dangers of worry. He talked and I listened, now it's your turn to listen.

There is nothing good about worry.

Worry is based on fear and the spirit of fear is not of Me. Worry is a thief that robs you of peace, joy, and confidence. It is life altering in the most negative way.

Worry is a death sentence; a sign of a lack of faith. It causes delays in your blessings and prohibits miracles. It is a dream snatcher, causing confusion. It is useless and can be contagious to those you love. Worry weakens you mentally, spiritually, physically, and emotionally and is a power being used against you. Worry stunts your mental, emotional, and spiritual growth and stops you from being all you were created to be. It diminishes potential, can destroy relationships, and damages your wings making it hard to not only fly but soar.

Worry is on the prowl to attach itself to those who will allow it. It can keep you in spectator mode watching everyone else live their lives. It can cause you to do things you might later regret (i.e. dwell on the past, be envious, be jealous, and hate). Worry can be a weight that is heavier than anything you have ever lifted. It can drain you of your energy, cause you to cancel plans, deny you of true love, and stink up your environment.

Worry can cause uncertainty; turning your "cans" into "cannots." It is an unapologetic destroyer that is prideful as it enhances your stress and creates nightmares. Its goal is to cause you to stumble. Worry is all around bad for you and your relationships.

What did I say?

Father, You said a mouth full and it was all good. Worry is not my friend, it is my enemy seeking to destroy me if I allow it. I must work to keep worry far from me and if the temptation arises, I must not give in to it. I must exercise my faith in You Lord. For as Joel Osteen shares, "When I worry, You rest and when I rest, You work."

Thoughts for you, the Reader. . .

Did you notice there were no pros to worry, only cons; even a little worry is unhealthy. Here is the moment to release your worry.

What do you worry about?

_____
_____
_____
_____

What has worry manifested in your life?

_____
_____
_____
_____

How long will you allow worry to steal from you and what will you do to stop it?

_____
_____
_____
_____

Worry

How do you intend to live your life going forward?

_____

_____

_____

_____

Today's Prayer: *Father, I confess that I haven't been depending on You as I should, instead, I have been doing things my way which have caused a lot of worry. Because You said it doesn't have to be in my life, I release it all now, in the name of Jesus. Help me live in peace.*

Today's Affirmation

(Say aloud)

I am Full of Peace

I am Patient

I am Capable of. . .(fill in the blank)

Write Your Vision

I decree and declare from this moment forward I will _____

_____

_____

_____

_____

_____

_____

_____

_____

_____

Day 7
Regret

"Regret is a feeling of sadness, repentance, sense of loss, disappointment, dissatisfaction over something that has happened or been done; remorse for a fault, act, a missed opportunity; a feeling of sorrow."
(Dictionary.com).

God is patient. He knows what we are made (Psalm 103:14). He is willing to forgive us and forget all our sins when we ask; all our regrets are thrown out (Isaiah 43:25), thank You, Jesus.

The problem isn't God remembering my sins, it's my memory of them and the accuser (devil) who is always on his job reminding me of them (Revelation 12:9-10). Read on for the revelation of my regret.

I have had so many regrets, and although I know they come as lessons that teach, for the longest time I only saw them as regret. As I talked to God about my experiences, I remember saying:

Regret sucks! I hate regretting, yet I do not know how not to do it. I keep going back in my mind to when things were good, or when I felt like I was on the right track. I keep seeing myself before my disappointments and failures and not seeing myself in my forgiveness and successes. God help me!

How do I break free or break through to a place of true forgiveness for myself? Why do I feel like I must suffer because of my failures and shortcomings? Why do I speak death and destructive words over myself just because I have not measured up to my definition of perfect? My eyes fill up with tears due to this pain that I have caused and the regrets I carry?

People tell me to "let go," but no one tells me how to do it. Why is it so hard for me to let go? Why do I have such a negative image of myself? I feel imprisoned by guilt. Why is guilt so strong? When will regret cease? How I long for the day when I stop replaying my mistakes detail by detail. When will the moment come when I truly let it all go?

Satan has done a number on you.

Stop listening to his lies. Do not give him control of your freedom. Who the Son sets free is free indeed and Jesus came to set you free (John 8:36). Forgiveness is for you, too, everybody makes mistakes, there is none that is perfect, or righteous, no not one (Romans 3:10). Do not be so hard on yourself. Every time you beat yourself up, your enemy laughs and the angels cry. Forgiveness is powerful. It is never too late to look yourself in the mirror and truly say, "I forgive you" and mean it. Every good thing starts with forgiveness, so do it for your sake, and do it for us. When you do not forgive yourself, you cause your loved ones to suffer because they are not getting the best of you. How unfair is that? Do not let all that Jesus did for you to be in vain. Tap into the truth, release the power within, and live. I am not mad at you.

Your perspective is off.

Listen to me and learn. What is so bad about learning about yourself? What is wrong with knowing your strengths and weaknesses and realizing you have a while to go to get to where you want to be? Why beat yourself up over weaknesses? You mean to tell me that you will not love yourself because you are not all that you thought you were? Why make the journey hard just because you do not understand it?

The more you hold on to the pain of the past, the less you care about the greatness of your future. You have been there and done that concerning your past, and if you want the opportunity to say that about your future, you have got to let it go. Let Me tell you something, "Eyes have not seen, neither ear heard, nor has it entered your heart what is in store for you" (1 Corinthians 2:9) when you let go of your past. Live in the now and work toward your future. Do not give up what you have yet to see because of mistakes you cannot seem to get over. Trust Me, it is not worth it. Regret not!

Let go of being perfect and
embrace that you are perfectly loved.

Regret is the start of a vicious cycle that brings along words you do not want to say and actions you do not want to do. You asked Me to help you, now listen to Me and take heed, "Let it go!" Let go of the regret and embrace the knowledge. You have learned some important things about yourself and you will continue to learn, so do not be upset or disappointed. Learn to love yourself for who you are so you can love yourself when you become who you want to be. You do not know everything you are going to go through, I do, and I still love what I see when I look at you!

Take a stand and fight for your life.

Give yourself a chance to live the life you want to live by breaking through from the life you have already lived. No more regrets, replaying every mistake you made and rehearsing your wrongs expecting them to turn out right. Let it go! Love yourself enough to let go of the pain of the past and enjoy the pleasures of the present. Focusing on what "was" is causing you to miss what "is," so stop it. Stop existing in the present while living in your past.

You asked how to break free and breakthrough. You do it by having a desire to forgive. Desire is a strong emotion. You feel it throughout your body, mind, and soul. You want it bad; that is what you need to break through, a real desire to forgive yourself. When you get there, the enemy of regret you will see no more.

Freedom awaits!

What is true forgiveness you are wondering? It is being okay with what happened or what did not happen. It is not changing the scenarios to have a different outcome. It is seeing yourself better because of the knowledge you learned about yourself. It is speaking life over yourself, your endeavors, and your life despite what you may call failures. It is laughing at the enemy of the situation instead of crying or feeling sad when it comes up. You made it through and you can help more people because of it.

Take a moment and think about Jesus, if they had known who He was and what His mission was, they would not have crucified Him (1 Corinthians 2:8). He now sits at My right hand in heaven interceding for you because He went through it. When the thought of failure comes up, remember who is bringing it to you and reject it with My Word. My Word never fails, it will put a smile on your face and a frown on the enemy's. Remind him of the Word in Romans 8:1 that says, "Now there is no condemnation for those who belong to Christ Jesus."

Your life is not over.
Will you endure for your promise?

It is time for you to live. What you were doing before was existing. You deserve to be happy and healthy. You deserve the true desires of your heart and you deserve what I have for you. Do you want it? I love you so much I sent your Elder Brother, Jesus to die for your sins (John 10:10). Because He died for your sins, you deserve to live. He did everything I asked Him to do so that you could live life abundantly. You deserve it.

Boldly cast your cares.

Acknowledgment is important. Do not lie to yourself and do not deceive others. You need Me! You can do nothing good without Me. The cares you carry are not meant for you to hold on to, you need to cast them to Me, because I care for you (1 Peter 5:7). You are not disqualified because of your past. Come boldly before My throne of grace and ask what you will (Hebrews 4:16). I love you and I want to hear from you. Have confidence in knowing I want great things for you and it gives Me great pleasure blessing you. Your blessings bring awareness of Me; I do not want to be your best-kept secret. Talk to Me, be honest, be bold, and be authentically you.

*Your good works will get noticed
and I will get the glory.*

An awareness of Me gives birth to curiosity and curiosity gives birth to seeking. With seeking comes finding and when they find Me, they find love and the realization that I have always loved them. That will be the moment they will love Me.

Love is powerful!

Love changes lives! Love does not discriminate. Love heals all wounds. Regret exits upon love's entrance, so you really do not need to regret a thing, you just need to love yourself.

What did I say?

Father, what I heard You say is I should let go of all my regrets. Regret doesn't come to serve me, it hinders and stifles me. You want me to stop listening to the lies of the devil who wants to control my freedom. You told me not to be so hard on myself and to forgive myself. Everyone has weaknesses as well as strengths and I am not to beat myself up because of weaknesses. I heard You say when true love enters regret will exit and that's what I will focus on, truly loving myself and not allowing my regrets to consume my being.

Thoughts for you, the Reader...

You heard my woes, have you any regrets, are you ready to let them go? The following questions are to help you get started in facing your regrets.

What is the purpose of regret?

_____

_____

_____

What can you do to make regret go away?

_____

_____

_____

How do you see your life with no regret?

_____

_____

_____

Regret

Review the scriptures for this day and record what God reveals to you.

Psalm 103:14

_____

_____

_____

Isaiah 43:25

_____

_____

_____

Revelation 12:9-10

_____

_____

_____

John 8:36

_____

_____

_____

What Did I Say?

Romans 3:10

1 Corinthians 2:9

1 Corinthians 2:8

Romans 8:1

Regret

John 10:10

1 Peter 5:7

Hebrews 4:16

Matthew 7:11

When you consider your regret(s), what do you hear God say?

Today's Prayer: *Thank You, Father, for Your love. Thank You for Your grace and mercy. Thank You for showing me how not to let regret control me, but to conquer it with self-love. I will not give control to negative thinking, but defeat it with Your Word, in Jesus' name, Amen.*

Today's Affirmations

(Say Aloud)

I am Forgiven

I am Chosen for Greatness

I am Capable of. . .(fill in the blank)

Write Your Vision

I decree and declare from this moment forward I will _____

_____

_____

_____

_____

_____

_____

_____

_____

_____

_____

Day 8
Trust

"Trust is the assured reliance on the character, ability, strength, or truth of someone or something; one in which confidence is placed."
(Merriam-Webster Dictionary)

God is trustworthy. The Bible is full of examples of people who trusted God to do exactly what He said He would do. Everyone He called for any reason was equipped for the task and provision was always provided.

I trusted God except during a season in my life where my mind was clogged full of negativity, doubt, despair, and confusion. It was a crazy time and what was the craziest is I knew better, I knew God loved me. Well, that season is over now, thank God. I have learned to go back to the basics and trust the One who never fails. Hopefully, as you continue to read, you will find revelation in my story.

Learn to trust.

God, I trust You, it's me I don't trust. You haven't given me a reason not to trust You, yet I know at times my actions are screaming distrust! It's really me that has issues with trust; You are just being God.

Sometimes when I hear instructions, cautions, or information, I question, "Is that me or You?" I've done things that seemed very much "You," but felt very much "me" and often wondered if it was the right thing to do. I second guess myself a lot and often worry all because I don't trust.

Knowledge is key to trusting.

A lack of trust comes from a lack of information, so what you do not trust is the information you have been given. This is an easy fix that can be solved with one word, "Study"! You have got to study for yourself so when questions are asked, you can answer with confidence (2 Timothy 2:15). When I speak to you, you will know it is Me and not you because you study the Bible and know the words you hear are aligned with the words you read. Studying will take you far in life.

Trust is not hard to do once you have done and continuously do your due diligence. If you do not trust people, it is because you are not paying attention to them or studying them as you should. If you do not trust yourself, the same basically applies. You are not paying attention to your life, your actions, and your triggers.

Pay attention and learn.

Your life is responding to you, so take inventory of what you are saying and how you are acting. Think about why you are behaving as you do and you will soon realize it is because you lack the trust in Me you need to live peaceably. What will it take to make you happy? Do you know?

There is a method to your madness.

Change your mind, change your life! Think on things that are good and praiseworthy (Philippians 4:8). If the thoughts you are thinking do not cause your face to smile, you are thinking of the wrong things. Get still, close your eyes, and see the life that you want. Open your eyes, verbalize it, thank

Me for it, and go get it! Only I know the end from the beginning and the beginning from the end, so if you are waiting for details or specific instructions to get started, My question to you is where is your faith? For faith is the substance of things hoped for, the evidence of things not seen (Hebrews 11:1). Begin walking and living your life in faith and there will not be an issue of trust.

Use your faith.

Without faith, it is impossible to please Me (Hebrews 11:6). Acknowledge Me in all your ways and let Me direct your path (Proverbs 3:6). I want you to believe that if you follow My lead, you can have and live the life you want. Having faith and using faith gives you the opportunity to grow it and see what it produces. Your life is not meant to be hard; it is meant to be exciting and enjoyable.

Believe and turn things around for yourself.

There must be a shift in your thinking before there can be outward change. Shift your focus, so that you can manifest what matters. You are power packed with what you need to produce everything your heart desires.

Take some time to get to know who you really are, not the person you have become, and trust that you can become the person you have always wanted to be. I know at this very moment you are thinking of reasons and excuses why you cannot become that person, and I am telling you to stop. Stop doing that to yourself and stop limiting Me. You are right about one thing; you do not trust; you do not trust because you do not believe.

Remember!

What happened to your faith? You used to be so bold and confident. Every word out of your mouth was positive. Now, when I listen to you I barely recognize you. Every word is doom and gloom, full of pessimism. What happened? Do you really think I do not love and care about you? I love you and it is time for you to start loving yourself again. No more crazy talk and self-sabotaging thoughts and actions.

Fight the good fight and win!

It is time for you to fight for your life! I do not mean to physically fight, I mean fight in faith. Have a violent faith, strong faith, faith like Jacob (Genesis 32:24), the type of faith that holds on until you receive the blessing you desire. You cannot have passive faith, (the type that is easily offended and quick to give up). What are you hoping for that you have yet to see? Can you be bold and in this very moment say it aloud? Faith speaks and I listen.

What did I say to you?

Father, You gave me the remedy for my lack of trust. You said I need to read and study, watch and pray. Trust is not hard to do when I pay attention. My faith, hope, and dreams can be restored when I change my mind and words about them. When I change my mind, my life will change. My focus has been off and my sight needs to be calibrated on the right things. Father, I can and will do better.

Thoughts for you, the Reader...

Can you relate to anything that was mentioned today? If you are ready to release your lack of trust and begin again, consider the following questions:

What happened to cause your lack of trust?

_____

_____

_____

_____

What event(s) happened to cause you to not trust God?

_____

_____

_____

_____

Review the scriptures given for this day and record what God reveals to you.

2 Timothy 2:15

Philippians 4:8

Hebrews 11:1

Hebrews 11:6

Proverbs 3:6

_____
_____
_____
_____

Genesis 32:24

_____
_____
_____
_____

2 Corinthians 5:7

_____
_____
_____
_____

When you consider your issue with trust, what do you hear God say?

_____
_____
_____
_____

Today's Prayer: *God, You know me better than I know myself, so I won't make any excuses. I repent right now for not trusting You and I apologize to myself. Help me to do better and to live my life in faith. Thank You! I ask for Your help in Jesus' name, Amen.*

Today's Affirmations

(Say Aloud)

I am Full of Faith

I am Peaceful

I am Capable of. . .(fill in the blank)

Write Your Vision

I decree and declare from this moment forward I will _____

_____

_____

_____

_____

_____

_____

_____

_____

_____

_____

Retaliate

Day 9
Fight Back

"To fight back is to attack or try to defeat someone who is attacking or trying to defeat oneself; to make a new effort against an opponent."
(Merriam-Webster Dictionary)

And from the days of John the Baptist, the kingdom of heaven suffers violence, and the violent taketh by force. (Matthew 11:12)

God is our vindicator. Dear friends, never take revenge. Leave that to the righteous anger of God. For the scripture says, "I will take revenge; I will pay them back," says the Lord (Romans 12:19 NLT). There is never a need to retaliate. God wants us to do our fighting in the spirit where it counts.

Think about it, when it comes to doing the things of God, there is always opposition. There is always someone speaking against you and/or your work; the thing you said you are called to do. I have experienced that a lot.

Below you will read His response to my shrinking for others, acting invisible, dimming my light, and acting like a chicken instead of soaring like an eagle. May your study lead you to new revelations. I had to change and thank God I did. My future is too bright and full of purpose and promise for me to relinquish it. Buckle up.

You have all you need.

I gave you everything you need to succeed and soar in life. Jesus gave you the keys to the Kingdom, but you are not using them. You are walking around weak when I made you strong. You are acting ignorant to My Word and My ways, yet you know them inside out. I speak to you and you speak to others as if we have never spoken. What is wrong with you? You are chosen for greatness, yet you wander in darkness. Why? You walk around afraid of the world, and I have equipped you to conquer, subdue, and overcome it.

Use your words.

I am tired of seeing you in the fetal position hiding in corners. You have too much power to walk around powerless. It is time for you to Wake Up from your way of life and start living. Jesus came that you would have life and have it more abundantly (John 10:10). You were never meant to live the way you are now living, but somewhere in your life you acknowledged and believed the lies and started living them.

Come back to the truth.

Jesus is the way and the truth (John 14:6). What He did for you is real as well as the benefits that come with it. You do not have to be sick; choose health instead. Remember, Jesus took stripes for your healing (Isaiah 53:5). If you believe in what He has done for you, walk out of sickness and into healing. He died for your sins and was bruised for every iniquity and generational curse, so be free from it all and walk His way.

Your words work; talk about what you want, not what you see. I saw nothing and created everything with My words;

you are equipped to do the same. What do you want to see? Life and death are in your tongue (Proverbs 18:21), choose to **speak life**.

Wake up!

Your life is not meant to be hard and you were not brought forth to live in sadness, so say "No" to it. Enough is enough of the lifestyle you have lived. There is so much more! I have a plan for you that will bless you in ways greater than you can imagine (1 Corinthians 2:8), but you must **fight back** and let go of your way to live it.

You are too precious to surrender to defeat.
Fight Back!

It is time to stop acting like you are less than great. If you cannot be who I created you to be with those around you, find others to be around. Your life is too precious and the assignment on your life is too important for you to blend in to be accepted. I created you to stand out!

What did I say?

Lord, what I heard You say is it's time for me to change. You have given me everything I need to succeed in this world and it's up to me to soar. You are tired of me acting ignorant of Your Word and neglecting the power I have in Jesus. You told me to use my words and live a great life and stop acting in ways that do not represent our relationship. I can't be extraordinary and ordinary at the same time, I must make a choice and from here on live that life.

Thoughts for you, the Reader...

Have you done this, acted less than you are to blend in? Were there times when you took a step back to watch and listen to yourself and literally shook your head? It really is the pits, living beneath your rights. It's time to fight back!

What has you acting less than great?

_____

_____

_____

_____

What is your biggest fear regarding being authentically you?

_____

_____

_____

_____

When you think about fighting back for the life God promised, what are your thoughts?

_____
_____
_____
_____
_____

What makes you mad enough to change?

_____
_____
_____
_____

Review the scriptures given for this day and record what God reveals to you.

Matthew 11:12

_____
_____
_____
_____

Romans 12:19

John 10:10

John 14:6

Isaiah 53:5

Proverbs 18:21

1 Corinthians 2:8

When you consider fighting back, what do you hear God say?

Today's Prayer: *Father, thank You for reminding me that I am wonderfully made by Your mighty hand. Forgive me for allowing the words and actions of others toward me to stop me from being extraordinary. I will no longer be a people pleaser. I will no longer allow the cares of this world to keep me from fulling the purpose and calling You have for my life. Thank You for the dream and for giving me all I need to pursue it.*

Today's Affirmations

(Say Aloud)

I am Courageous

I am Purpose Driven

I am Capable of. . .(fill in the blank)

Write Your Vision

I decree and declare from this moment forward I will _____

_____
_____
_____
_____
_____
_____
_____
_____
_____
_____

Day 10
Forgive and Forget

> "To forgive is to cease to feel resentment against (an offender); or claim to requital, to grant relief from payment."
> *(Merriam-Webster Dictionary)*

God forgives! God is so merciful. He is longsuffering towards us, and because He is, the goal is that we extend the same to ourselves and to others. Everyone makes mistakes. What we do after the mistake further tells the story of the mistake.

One of my traits is that of a perfectionist; however, it doesn't always serve me in the best way. At times, it makes forgiving and forgetting a challenge. As you read my conversation with God, you will soon see what I mean by perfectionist. Hopefully, a blessing is hidden in it for you.

It starts with forgiveness.

Lord, one of the challenging things for me has been to forgive those who have wronged me and that includes myself. Sometimes, I sit and think about those things and when I finally stop thinking about them, years have passed. I have wasted so much time in regret and thinking of circumstances that would have had different outcomes. In my mind, I rewind the clock, but time still moves forward. I am stuck!

I am stuck because I knew better. I was smarter than the way I acted, and I allowed things to happen because I did not fight back! I was like a sheep left to the shearer; stripped of my dignity. I was powerful but acted powerless, knowledgeable but acted stupid, protected but felt unprotected. I knew better and I disappointed myself, but what's worse, I disappointed You.

You were talking to me, sending me signs, I recognized them as signs but still acted weak. I did not respond to the help You sent. I am ashamed of myself. It is hard to shake that off but harder holding on to it. I am stuck! Lord, help me to overcome this shame and make it a footstool in my life.

You will rejoice again!

I have given you everything you need to get over this including a promise of giving you double for your shame (Isaiah 61:7), yet you are still holding on to it. The problem is you do not believe Me and you do not trust My love. I love you and you being hard on yourself will never change My love for you.

Nothing is hidden from Me!

Would it help if I told you I saw it happen before it happened? I see your joy, pain, happiness, and disappointments. I know you. Nothing is hidden from Me, not your strengths nor your weaknesses. I know from what you are made. I know who you are and whose you are. Do you? It is you that has forgotten. You forgot how much I love you, that I made you and ultimately died for you. The moment you asked for forgiveness, I forgave and forgot about it, but you did not. You did not follow My lead. Instead, you allowed yourself to be led astray by the lies of the enemy. Do as I have done, forgive and forget. There are no wasted moments, all things will work together for your good because you love Me (Romans 8:28). So, let it go and live!

You worried about the wrong thing.

You spent too many years focusing on what happened back then, so much so that you are missing the now moments. You allowed guilt, fear, and shame to paralyzed you because you would not let it go. I am not mad at you! I do not think about your mistakes, I think about your purpose.

Suddenly, you got up!

I have seen you let it go and live. I have seen your life straighten out in the most beautiful way. I know your life will be fulfilled. I know it because I saw the day you finally believed. You were sick and tired of being sick and tired and you surrendered. You decided to cast all your cares (1 Peter 5:7) on Me and allowed Me to be God. You released the false notion of being perfect, as you remembered there is none perfect/righteous, no not one (Romans 3:10).

The weapons of warfare are not carnal.

I am perfection. I saw you change your mind, words, and actions. It changed your life. I am not worried about your yesterday; I know your today and rejoice about your tomorrow. The enemy was working to steal, kill, and destroy you (John 10:10). His suggestions got the best of you for years, but you finally began to fight back and overcome. You are the winner in this scenario because you fought back. You no longer took the abuse of the enemy, you fought back with My Word and your actions, and now you are victorious.

A word from Me can change your life.

You had to get to a point in life when you really believed to be able to see that all things are possible. I know you believed in different moments in your life, but this last battle you were in, caused you to doubt. Your doubts and fears were prominent while your faith was diminishing. You sought counsel in everyone but Me, then when you came to Me, you doubted My response.

You began praying in fear and not in faith. You lost your confidence and boldness and lived in depression and sadness. I watched you suffer because of your doubt and I saw you die. The person I created was no longer recognizable until that moment you remembered.

You remembered who you are and whose you are. You realized the way you were living your life was not My best for you and you wanted the promise. You believed again and because you did, you began to live again, and this time you lived it more abundantly!

The past is gone with every dumb decision you made so no longer dwell on it. Do not look back if looking back makes you sad; only look back as a frame of reference to give Me praise! I love you. My love will get you through anything. My love never fails. Trust Me and the love I have for you; it is real, and nothing compares to it. Do not waste any more time in regret. Learn life's lessons and live!

What did I say?

Father, You told me to let go of my past mistakes and live the good life that awaits me. You said You will give me

Forgive and Forget

double for my trouble. You know everything that has happened; there is nothing hidden from You. You are a good Father who forgives and forgets and I need to do the same. Holding grudges is unhealthy.

Thoughts for you, the Reader...

Did you see the mess I was in? Did you see the perfectionist traits come out, not wanting to make mistakes, wanting everything to be just right? Did you notice the time wasted? That was my story, now it's time for you to share yours and get free.

What has happened to you that you find hard to forgive?
_____
_____
_____
_____
_____

What happens when you hold on to hurt?
_____
_____
_____
_____
_____

How will you forgive those who hurt you?

_____
_____
_____
_____
_____

How will you forgive yourself for what you allowed?

_____
_____
_____
_____
_____

Review the scriptures given for this day and record what God reveals to you.

Isaiah 61:7

_____
_____
_____
_____
_____

Romans 8:28

1 Peter 5:7

Romans 3:10

John 10:10

Regarding forgiving and forgetting, what is God saying to you?

_____

_____

_____

_____

Today's Prayer: *Thank You, Lord, for teaching me how to forgive and forget. You have shown me the power in forgiving others especially in forgiving myself. I repent for holding people as well as myself hostage to unforgiveness. It's okay if they never apologize, I release everyone right now in Jesus' name. I will no longer allow unforgiveness to bind me.*

Today's Affirmations

(Say Aloud)

I am Merciful

I am Full of Grace

I am Capable of. . .(fill in the blank)

Write Your Vision

I decree and declare from this moment forward I will _____

_____

_____

_____

_____

_____

_____

_____

_____

_____

_____

Shift

Day 11
I Want to Change

"To change is to make different in some particular; to give a different position, course or direction to; to make a shift from one to another; to replace with another."
(Merriam-Webster Dictionary)

God is able! He can do exceeding abundantly above all we can ask or think according to the power that works within us (Ephesians 3:20).

Life is an adventure, it's like the craziest roller coaster we will ever ride. At times, it's fun and other times it's scary and can make you dizzy and discombobulated. That's what happened to me. I changed from good to seemingly bad according to my standards and wanted to go back to my normal and be what I considered good again. Below is a sneak peek into my conversation with God, I pray you are blessed by it. Buckle up.

Change your mind and your actions will follow.

God, I have been mean, hateful, quick to anger, quick to speak, and quick to hold grudges. This has been my way for a very long time and I don't enjoy it. When I act like this, it isn't my best. In fact, it's probably my worse and no one deserves that, not even me. I want to change! I don't want this to be a part of my personality anymore. I want to be better.

You can do whatever you want.

I'm not like this all the time, however, it's those times when I am that brings forth sadness. I want to change. I know You have a great plan for my life heavenly Father and Your thoughts for me are good and not evil (Jeremiah 29:11). I want to live in that space. I want to do as the Bible says and be angry but not sin (Ephesians 4:26). I don't want to hold grudges and make my home miserable because of my negative attitude. Walking around quiet and not speaking isn't how I should be. It's not right and no one deserves it, especially the ones I love. I want to stop being so easily offended. Where did that spirit come from anyway? Where and when was that seed planted? I want to be a peacemaker (Matthew 5:9), loving and kind to everyone, especially my family. I don't want to be known as the angry person, the one who will snap in a moment's notice causing the family to have to walk lightly around me. I don't want to be that person anymore; I want to change. Why do I get so offended? Why do I take things so personally? Why do I act this way? What's wrong with me?

Take responsibility.

No one owes me anything. If I am honest, my fits come from me being disappointed in myself. My goals and dreams were once so big and bright and when I didn't do what it took to accomplish them, I got mad. The way I felt on the inside began to show on the outside and no one is to blame but me. There it is, full responsibility, help me to change. I understand that it's the little foxes that spoil the vine (Song of Solomon 2:15). My ways have messed me up and broken me down, but You, oh God, are the fixer, nothing is too hard for You. Help me change.

Without a vision, people perish.

You stopped believing in yourself and began focusing on the wrong things. You focused and dwelled on things that made you sick and angry until your actions made you unhappy. You are what happened. You broke your stride and only you can fix it. You allowed your mind to experience the worse, now give yourself the opportunity to experience the best. Free your mind of the negative images that are causing you to walk in fear and give it permission to soar. Imagine and build the life you really want. Forgive yourself for all the reckless thinking and think again. This time think of things that are lovely, kind, praise-worthy, virtuous, things from above and of good report (Philippians 4:8).

Think on things that matter!

Leave the past where it is and walk towards your purpose and possibilities. It is time to turn your "cannots into cans" and all your dreams into plans. Remember, if you can believe, all things are possible (Mark 9:23). I am an abundant God and you can have, be, and do whatever you allow yourself to believe. I am in control. Ask and you will receive (Matthew 7:7).

Speak Life!

Can you talk about it? Does the conversation of your vision roll off your tongue easily or is there hesitation because of doubt? Shake off doubt and despair and put on faith and confidence. Frame your world with your conversation, talk about it until you see and have it. Life is not meant to be hard. You have made it hard because you did not believe the truth concerning Me. I love you and care, so fear not and know that I will never leave or forsake you (Hebrews 13:5).

Only Believe!

I will cause all things to work together for your good (Romans 8:28). I will cause you to walk above and never again beneath, to lend and not borrow, to be first and not last (Deuteronomy 28:13, Deuteronomy 15:6). I will bless you and cause you to live an abundant life. I can and will do more than you can ever imagine. I created you! I have seen you throughout your life. Nothing is hidden from Me. I know you! So, when you ask Me to help you, please know that I will and that I am helping you even when you do not see it. Run to Me, not from Me!

What did I say?

God, what I heard You say is I stopped believing in myself and began focusing on the wrong thing and You are right. I broke my stride and only I can fix it. I allowed my mind to experience the worse, now it's time for me to experience the best. You told me to leave the past where it is and walk with purpose towards my future. You said all things are possible when I believe, and I need to speak life. I must do my part by changing my mind, my words, and my actions so that my life can change. If I want to change, I can change.

I Want to Change

Thoughts for you, the Reader...

We all have room to grow, what adjustments are you willing to make? What needs to change about you?

_____

_____

_____

_____

What do you think the hardest part of change will be for you?

_____

_____

_____

_____

What possibilities can you imagine?

_____

_____

_____

_____

What Did I Say?

What past actions impacted your future goals?

_____
_____
_____

What will you do to protect your goals going forward?

_____
_____
_____

Review the scriptures given for this day and record what God reveals to you.

Ephesians 3:20

_____
_____
_____

Jeremiah 29:11

_____
_____
_____

I Want to Change

Ephesians 4:26

Matthew 5:9

Song of Solomon 2:15

Philippians 4:8

Mark 9:23

Matthew 7:7

Hebrews 13:5

Romans 8:28

I Want to Change

Deuteronomy 28:13

_____
_____
_____
_____

Deuteronomy 15:6

_____
_____
_____
_____

When you consider the changes you must make to become your best self, what did you hear God say?

_____
_____
_____
_____

Today's Prayer: *Thank You, Father, for loving me and giving me the tools to change. I take responsibility for where I am now and I will be responsible for where I am going. I know change is waiting for me to set my mind in the right direction and I do it now, in the name of Jesus! I remove every trigger that has a hold on me with the authority given to me by Jesus. Thank You for causing me to look in my mirror for the problem and the solution.*

I Want to Change

Today's Affirmation

(Say Aloud)

I am My Solution

I am Responsible

I am Capable of. . .(fill in the blank)

Write Your Vision

I decree and declare from this moment forward I will _____

_____
_____
_____
_____
_____
_____
_____
_____
_____
_____
_____

Day 12
In My Way

> "Way: a method, plan, or means for attaining a goal;
> a direction or vicinity."
> (*Merriam-Webster Dictionary*)

Have you ever felt like you were in your own way and in God's way? It's so easy to think we are doing the right thing, be loud about it, but be wrong. God talked to me about the self-sabotaging things that were once a part of my life. He was right as always. I was very guilty of allowing fear to make me pump the brakes. I have gotten better, thank God, and am no longer a best-kept secret. When God speaks, we should listen. Enjoy.

Without Faith...

You know Lord, sometimes I wonder if what You've shown me will ever be, and then I think again and believe. I believe in what was spoken over me. I believe in You, I believe in Your Word, and with everything I can, I believe in me.

All things are possible when you believe.

Do you really believe in yourself? I know you believe in Me, but do you really believe in you? You keep getting in My way! Every time I am ready to promote you or show you something concerning what I want you to do, you get in My way. Your fear of rejection, fear of judgment, and fear of failing is prevalent.

Why are you afraid to walk in the faith I have given you? Why do you think I show you so much? Do you really think it is to tease you? I show you a lot because your faith is big enough to receive it, but without the actions needed, you will not obtain it.

Move!

Get out of your own way. Stop sabotaging the dream I gave you. You can have it all if you add work to your faith (James 2:14-26). Everything I showed you is yours, plus a lot of what I did not (1 Corinthians 2:9). You must move out of your way and into position. Stop living in the nightmare and wake up to the dream.

Jesus did, so you could do!

Give yourself a chance to live life abundantly. Give yourself a chance to soar and give yourself a chance to make a lot of people proud. Be bold, take a leap of faith, and let Me see you work. While you are working, remember, all things are possible. The risk of not taking a risk is so much greater than taking it.

Only Believe!

Believe again in the possibilities that once bombarded your mind. See yourself higher than you have ever been; break records, set records, make your impossibilities everyday activities. Wake up excited and go to bed satisfied. You can prevent the nightmares in your head by living an authentic life. Do you think it is a coincidence that the people who see and talk to you all say the same thing about you? It is not. It is confirmation after confirmation and you know it. Move out of your way! Make no more excuses, it is time for the real you to show up and live.

What did I say?

Father, what I heard You tell me is to stop sabotaging my progress and walk in the gift of faith. You said every time You want to do something amazing for me, I get in Your way. My fear is obvious and I need to conquer it now. I need to give myself a chance to live an abundant life and start taking risks. I need to get out of Your way and get out of my own way. I need to believe again in **me**!

Thoughts for you, the Reader...

Do you sabotage your progress? Consider the following questions:

What are some of your experiences of getting in your way and in God's way?

_____

_____

_____

_____

How do your beliefs impact your personal road blocks?

_____

_____

_____

_____

What do you need to do to get out of your way?

_____

_____

_____

_____

What Did I Say?

Now that the truth is revealed, what will you do?

_____
_____
_____
_____
_____

Review the scriptures given for this day and record what God reveals to you.

James 2:14-26

_____
_____
_____
_____
_____

1 Corinthians 2:9

_____
_____
_____
_____
_____

When you consider being in the way of your blessing, what do you hear God say?

_____

_____

_____

_____

Today's Prayer: *Thank You, Lord for showing me the error of my ways. I submit my will and my ways to You, for You know all things. I believe You want me to succeed in every area of my life. Forgive me for getting in Your way. I will do better. I will no longer allow my way of doing things nor my lack of understanding of Your ways stop me from fulfilling the purpose and calling You have for my life.*

Today's Affirmations
(Say Aloud)

I am Ready to Soar

I am Courageous

I am Capable of. . .(fill in the blank)

Write Your Vision

I decree and declare from this moment forward I will _____

_____
_____
_____
_____
_____
_____
_____
_____
_____
_____

Day 13
Empower Yourself

"Empower is to give official authority or legal power to; enable; to promote the self-actualization or influence of."
(Merriam-Webster Dictionary)

God is all power! He can do all things but fail. God is gracious and strategic; He knows who we need, what we need, and when we need it. His best plan for us was Jesus. God did it all for us and gave us all that we need to live and thrive on earth.

The Bible is full of life-changing information. I remember reading and applying its principles long ago. During that time my life seemed magical. Sure, there were times when it rained, the thunder roared, and the lightning struck, but somehow my faith allowed me to endure those moments graciously.

Fast forward, I began listening to negativity and began questioning what I knew. God lovingly reminded me of my ability to not only encourage myself but to empower myself. In the Bible, David encouraged himself when things got bad

(1 Samuel 30:6). I can do the same. His reminder blessed me and released me from the stronghold of those negative words and my negative thoughts. Read on and see how I was blessed.

Oh, yes you can!

You have everything you need to empower yourself, so do it! Do not wait for someone to do what you are equipped to do. Put yourself in places to listen and learn. Turn off distractions so you can turn on possibilities. You have got to do what it takes to have the life you want.

Do you know what you want?

What type of life do you want? How does it look to you? Can you envision people seeing your good works and glorifying Me, the Father (Matthew 5:16)? How long will you make us wait? When will your Day One of creating the best you begin? Are you satisfied with your life, should I just be quiet and leave you alone? Am I pushing you too hard? Look around, can you honestly say that you do not see the need?

Everyone has a purpose and yours is staring right back at you, so do something and do it now.

What's your plan?

You must see it mentally before you seize it physically! Write your vision down and make it plain and legible so that when you read it, you will hop, jump or leap into action (Habakkuk 2:2). Your vision must be so precise and so magnificent that you begin to smile while writing. It has got to be so out there that you blush and for a split-second think to yourself, "Really?" and then say to yourself, "Yes, really!"

Embrace your abilities.

It is time to look in the mirror, put your shoulders back, lift your head up, and embrace your own abilities. You are well able to encourage yourself, so do it. You are empowered to become all your heart desires. Release the need to be pumped and primed by people and go to work.

What did I say?

Father, I heard You say that I am equipped with what I need to empower myself. I do not have to wait for others to do for me what I am able to do. I have got to get a vision for my life and write down my plan, my goals, my dreams, and go after them. I have power to live a great and abundant life and it's up to me to do it. I can do this work.

Thoughts for you, the Reader...

Let's get everything God has promised. Let's not let Jesus' sacrifice be in vain for our lives. Let's live abundantly like He said we could. Let's go get it, let's go for the gold, and endure for our promise! Day one starts **now**. Get ready, get set, go, and don't look back!

What makes you happy?
_____
_____
_____
_____

What do you see yourself doing in this season of your life?
_____
_____
_____
_____
_____

How do you feel about the changes you have to make?

___

Review the scriptures given for this day and record what God reveals to you.

1 Samuel 30:6

___

Matthew 5:16

___

Habakkuk 2:2

When you consider empowering yourself, what do you hear God say?

Today's Prayer: *Heavenly Father, You have equipped me to soar in life. During times when I feel down or feel like I can't do something You tell me I can, so I will encourage myself. I will accept the encouragement of others when I receive it, however, I won't run after it. I will do as You say. I will live and prosper in Jesus' name, Amen.*

Today's Affirmation

(Say Aloud)

I am Creative

I am Empowered

I am Capable of. . .(fill in the blank)

Write Your Vision

I decree and declare from this moment forward I will _____

_____

_____

_____

_____

_____

_____

_____

_____

_____

_____

Day 14
Attention

> "Attention is the act or state of applying the mind to something; a condition of readiness involving especially a selective narrowing or focusing of consciousness and receptivity."
> (*Merriam-Webster Dictionary*)

When I think of paying attention to what's important, the first biblical person who comes to mind is Noah. God gave Noah specific instructions for building the ark (Genesis 6), and if Noah wasn't paying attention to detail, we may have ended up reading a different outcome.

When I make up my mind to do something, I will see it through until the end. However, moments when my mind isn't set, it wanders, and nothing gets accomplished. There were seasons in my life when I couldn't seem to focus on anything productive. My thoughts were so crazy and foolish that soon my actions began to follow. I was in a rollercoaster of emotions during that time. I had to make changes in my thought process to see better outcomes in myself, my relationships, my projects, and my world.

Our Heavenly Father does not want us hurting ourselves. He does and says whatever it takes to get us back on track to living the life He sent us forth to live. As you continue in your reading, you will see His directives to me.

Are you focused?

Are you paying attention to your thoughts, what you are dwelling on and imagining? Consider your situation and surroundings, including your friends and those with whom you spend most of your time. Is your conversation edifying? Are you collectively striving for excellence? Are some getting better while others are getting bitter? You are chosen for greatness, so playtime is over; I have need of you.

Change your mind and words.

Is what you desire and the words that come out of your mouth in agreement? Look at your life and answer that question. Your life is an image of your words. What has been the subject of your conversation? You know how I know you have been snared by your words (Proverbs 6:2)? It is because you keep talking about the same thing over and over. You keep asking Me to fix what has been fixed and you act as if it has not been fixed, after you asked. You have allowed fear to come in and you need to remove it from your life.

Life is a journey.

I am not saying you cannot enjoy your life and have moments of extreme pleasure and laughter because you can. I want you to be happy and I love seeing you smile. I want you to have your heart's desires. Are you satisfied with where you are now? You can have more and live your life on a different level if you want. Let your mind take you to the place of your dreams; for where the mind goes, the body will follow. Are you ready to soar? Your season of barely getting by is over. The thoughts I have for you are good and not evil, so raise your level of expectation. I come to give you an expected end (Jeremiah 29:11) what are you expecting?

Just believe!

Fear and faith cannot coexist. To have the things you want, you must choose faith and firmly kick fear out of your life. Do you ever wonder why it seems your negative confession works more and at times quicker than your positive confession? It is because you believe the negative and doubt the positive.

When it comes to your negative thoughts, you focus on and put energy into them. You are supposed to put your energy and expectation in what you want to manifest—the positive things and not in doubt and negativity. Feed what you want to grow and starve what you want to die.

If you want the things that make you happy to manifest, feed them with positive words, affirmations, visualization, and expectation. Starve the negative by speaking life to the positive. Change what you believe and have a different experience.

Believe good things will happen for you and they will. Profess the good you desire and believe in it and you will soon see the manifestation of your belief. No matter how small your faith is, it is strong (Matthew 17:20).

When you change your mind, your life will change!

You are a mind shift away from the change you want to experience. Ask yourself, "Are the thoughts I am thinking what I want to manifest?" If they are, good, and if they are not, silence them by speaking life to what you want. One of the secrets to living good is thinking great. Your mind is powerful. Just like you can think yourself out of a situation, you can also think yourself into it.

Think good thoughts!

Guard your heart and mind with all diligence and think on things that edify, build you up, are of a good report, and are praiseworthy (Philippians 4:8). Bad news is not praiseworthy and negative thinking can produce bad news. Let the mind of Christ be in you (Philippians 2:5). Christ has a winning mind, a miracle producing mind, a lovely mind, and an "all things are possible" mind. The mind of Christ is a grateful mind, an obedient mind, it is honorable and praiseworthy. Lose your mind and let this (a Christ-like) mind lead you instead. The mind of Christ is the ultimate mind.

You were created to live abundantly!

Your life and those who are watching will either thank you or rebuke you, bless you or curse you, promote you or demote you. Something will happen, and you have the power to determine what it is. I speak blessings over you, blessings and not curses, you will live and not die; you will produce much fruit and live a satisfied life. Change your mind and your life will change. I love you!

What did I say?

Lord, what I heard You say is that part of my responsibility to living an abundant life is having a Christ-like mind. I need to pay attention to my thoughts and imagine good things. My life is an image of my words. You love me and Your thoughts toward me are good and not evil. You said faith and fear cannot coexist so I choose faith. I must starve what I want to die and feed what I want to grow, that means to starve my fear and feed my faith. When I believe that good things will happen for me, they will begin to happen.

Attention

Thoughts for you, the Reader...

Consider the winning, miracle-producing mindset of Christ and allow it to lead you into an abundant life.

What's on your mind?

_____
_____
_____

What recent manifestations have your mind produced?

_____
_____
_____

How many times have you stopped or pumped the brake on your good ideas because of doubt and negative thoughts that you believed?

_____
_____
_____

What were those ideas?

_____
_____
_____
_____

Now that you have written them down, what do you intend to do with them?

_____
_____
_____
_____

The next time a negative thought comes to your mind, what will you do with it?

_____
_____
_____
_____

Review the scriptures given for this day and record what God reveals to you.

Genesis 6

___

Proverbs 6:2

___

Jeremiah 29:11

___

Matthew 17:20

Philippians 4:8

Philippians 2:5

When you consider the things that have your attention, what did you hear God say?

Today's Prayer: *Thank You, Lord, for loving me so much and letting me know that all is not lost. The bad things I manifested in the past can be reversed to good and my life can be spectacular going forward if I renew my mind and think on things that matter. I realize my mind is powerful and I want to use it to bless me. I let go of the negative events of my past in Jesus' name!*

Today's Affirmations
(Say Aloud)

I am a Positive Thinker

I am Focused

I am Capable of. . .(fill in the blank)

Write Your Vision

I decree and declare from this moment forward I will _____

_____
_____
_____
_____
_____
_____
_____
_____
_____
_____

Day 15
Celebrate

> "Celebrate is to perform (a sacrament or solemn ceremony) publicly and with appropriate rites; to honor (an occasion) especially by solemn ceremonies or by refraining from ordinary business; to mark (something) by festivities or other deviation from routine; to hold up or play up for public notice"
> *(Merriam-Webster Dictionary)*

God is worthy of praise! You can read countless accounts in the Bible when celebrations took place because of the awesome wonders of God. Those in the Bible gave us a peek into the miracles and joy of praising God.

God is worthy of celebrating! Sometimes, all it takes is for a word to stand out in the Bible to change your whole situation. For me, I didn't always know when to celebrate nor did I think I had a reason, but God told me different. He reminded me of the endless reasons to celebrate. Let the praise begin.

You are wonderfully made and uniquely beautiful.

Learn to celebrate who you are right now. Celebration does not start with what is happening outside of you; it starts with what is happening on the inside. You should always be celebrating because, within you, something is always happening. When you learn, grow, receive revelation, change your mind, develop, and do anything positive, celebrate! These and so many other things are reasons to celebrate.

You matter!

If you take the time to celebrate yourself, you will not have time for self-sabotage. Celebrating yourself makes you less dependent on others to celebrate you. When you are independent of praise from others, their criticism of you loses power. There will be no more emotional instability when you see yourself as the one who matters.

Celebrate You!

When was the last time you took a good look at yourself and smiled? Maybe you do not think you have anything to smile about, but in this very moment, take a deep breath, now let it out. You have a reason to smile and so much to celebrate. Learn to love, smile, and even laugh at yourself. Learn all about the incredible you and celebrate! It is time to truly embrace your uniqueness! Forget what others do not understand about you and do not alter My creation to fit their opinion of you. You were handcrafted by Me and I made no mistake; so, embrace My creation! Believe you are loved and learn to love. Love is powerful and it never fails.

Listen!

I love you! Everything you need is waiting for you to shift to praise instead of pout. Your praise will do wonders in your life. It has the power to change your perspective and literally change your life. Do not let what you see, feel or where you are stop you from praising Me. In an instant, things can change. In an instant, things will change! Celebrate and give

Me praise, for if you choose to keep silent, the rocks will cry out, (Luke 19:40). Let everything that has breath, praise Me (Psalm 150:6).

Believe!

Get your mind off the lies, the misunderstandings, and the persecutions and put it on the truth. The truth is you are fearfully and wonderfully made (Psalm 139:14), a unique piece of My workmanship. You were made perfectly in My image. I did not create you with more of something and less of another, you have everything you need. When I finished, I looked at you and said, "It is good!" You are good and a part of you is your personality, so be who I created you to be and you will see My best.

What did I say?

Father, what I heard You say is I should always celebrate my life. Something awesome is happening for me within no matter what I currently see. When I celebrate my life, I won't make time to sabotage it. I need to love myself unconditionally and not loving myself shows my lack of appreciation for what You created. With every breath I take, I have a reason to celebrate. It's not about the big or small things, it's about life itself and You Lord, the Creator. My life is worthy to be praised.

Thoughts for you, the Reader. . .

Have you had moments when you dimmed your light to make those around you feel good? If you have experienced any of what you have just read and are ready to let go of the weight of others, consider the following questions:

What do you celebrate about you?

_____
_____
_____
_____

What do you view as unique about you?

_____
_____
_____
_____

How do you embrace your uniqueness?

_____
_____
_____
_____

Celebrate

What makes you smile?

Review the scripture given for this day and record what God reveals to you.

Luke 19:40

Psalm 150:6

Psalm 139:14

When you consider celebrating yourself, what do you hear God say?

_____

_____

_____

_____

Today's Prayer: *Thank You, Father, for reminding me that I am not a mistake. I realize I am wonderfully and uniquely made by Your mighty hand. I ask You to take away the impulse to people please in the name of Jesus. I love who I am, I love how I look, and I will no longer self-sabotage. I will celebrate my uniqueness and celebrate my life. I am getting better and better every day in every way and I will celebrate, in Jesus' name, Amen.*

Celebrate

Today's Affirmations

(Say Aloud)

I am Enlightened

I am Special

I am Capable of. . .(fill in the blank)

Write Your Vision

I decree and declare from this moment forward I will _____

_____

_____

_____

_____

_____

_____

_____

_____

_____

_____

Day 16
Let God Arise

> "Arise is to come into being or to attention;
> to originate from a source; to get up or stand up;
> to move upward; ascend"
> *(Merriam-Webster Dictionary)*

God is high and lifted up (Isaiah 57:15). He is magnificent in all His ways. He can do all things, for He is the great Creator. Nothing is too hard for our true and living God (Jeremiah 10:10).

There was a time when I magnified my problems over my God. I don't like admitting that, but it's true. My actions were dominated by worry, fear, and frustration. I have always known that God is almighty, however, and this is no excuse, I let my situations and circumstances rule.

That time has passed, thank God, and I boldly say, I no longer magnify problems, I magnify my God. I chose to let God arise in my life and all His enemies in my life be scattered (Psalm 68:1). As you continue to read, I pray you receive revelation and completely let God arise!

There is nobody greater than God. He is the Alpha and the Omega, the beginning and the end. He spoke this world into existence and created man from dust; who is like our God. The Bible tells us in Philippians 2:10-11, "At the name of Jesus every knee will bow, in heaven and on earth and under the earth and every tongue declare that Christ is Lord, to the glory of God the Father" (NLT). Let God Arise!

I Am who you need.

I Am the connection you need, the hook-up that you want, and the favor of which you ask. You are going around asking people who they know that does whatever it is you need when you know Me. If you let Me arise in your life, problems are solved. I have the answer to all your questions and the solutions to all you will encounter. I know what you need (Philippians 4:19). Jesus is not dead (Matthew 28:6) and asking in His name is powerful.

I Am true and living!

Let Me arise in your life! Greet Me upon awakening and thank Me at day's end. Respect and honor Me for who I am; your Heavenly Father, Creator of Heaven and earth. I am the one who spoke this world into existence (Genesis 1). Let Me arise in your life so the enemies in your life can be scattered.

I am not like man/woman!

Consider the comparison of some of the characteristics of God and man.

God	Mankind
Right	Wrong
Selfless	Selfish
Love is unconditional and pure	Love is with conditions
Kind and patient	Short tempered and mean
Forgives all the time	Forgives sometimes
Knows the future	Knows nothing

You have work to do. When you understand how I feel about the enemies in your life, you will not tolerate them. Speak to your mountain and tell it to move, and then **you** take action. Do the work I have asked you to do and watch them scatter. Turn the light on in all the dark areas of your life and expose them to the truth. There is a real enemy whose desire is to steal, kill, and destroy you (John 10:10), do not let him do it. Let Me arise!

What did I say?

Lord, You said that my messes could be alleviated when I let You arise in my life. I have the power to speak to my mountains and command them to move. You are who I need and there is never a time when I need to go searching for favors. All I need to do is talk to You. I need to acknowledge You when I wake up and thank You before going to bed. I need to show You that I trust You by letting You arise in every area of my life.

Thoughts for you, the Reader...

It's time to follow or begin to follow the Holy Spirit, the real leader and let Him lead and guide you in all truth. Consider the following questions:

What is the area in your life where you have taken control?

_____
_____
_____
_____

What has your control caused to surface or appear that is unwarranted?

_____
_____
_____
_____

What Did I Say?

What has the enemy stolen that you want back?

_____

_____

_____

_____

How do you plan to fight for what you want?

_____

_____

_____

_____

What will you do differently to make this a lifestyle change and not just an event?

_____

_____

_____

_____

Review the scriptures given for this day and record what God reveals to you.

Isaiah 57:15

_____
_____
_____
_____
_____

John 10:10

_____
_____
_____
_____

Psalm 68:1

_____
_____
_____
_____
_____

Philippians 4:19

_____
_____
_____
_____

Matthew 28:6

_____
_____
_____
_____

Genesis 1

_____
_____
_____
_____

When you consider letting God arise in your life, what did you hear God say?

_____
_____
_____
_____

Today's Prayer: *Father, I now realize I have allowed the enemy to oppress me in many ways. It stops now. I will no longer listen to his lies and received his suggestions. I believe in You! I believe You love me, I believe Jesus died for my sins, and I believe You raised Him from the dead. I believe He took every negative thing that was meant for me to the cross and said, "It is finished!" I believe I can be free indeed and I accept my freedom in Jesus' name.*

Today's Affirmation

(Say Aloud)

I am Free

I am Enlightened

I am Capable of. . .(fill in the blank)

Write Your Vision

I decree and declare from this moment forward I will _____

_____

_____

_____

_____

_____

_____

_____

_____

_____

Day 17
Can My Dream Still Manifest?

> "A dream is a series of thoughts, images, or emotions [one can be asleep or awake]."
> *(Merriam-Webster Dictionary)*

God is a communicator! He knows how to talk to His children and how to get our attention. His love for us never fails.

Today, I share how I allowed fear of my spoken words to get the best of me. I have wasted so much time being unproductive and complainßing about things that were not worth my energy or access into my life. In one moment, I would dream about my dream and in another, I would complain because I was not living it. I spent years in spectator mode watching others' dreams become reality. I watched, admired, and sometimes envied.

Can my dream still happen?

After all, I have done and said against myself and my dream I often wonder, is it too late for me or can it still take place? My words and my actions are what scare me the most with regards to my dreams becoming a reality. I know that life and death are in the power of the tongue and my words were not always good (Proverbs 18:21).

Miracles happen when you believe.

The thoughts and plans I have for you are all good. Although you spoke foolishly for years, your desire to see your dreams become real is a part of what is needed to manifest them. Is it too late you ask? No, it is never too late when you believe. Did your death words cause damage you ask? They slowed you down and prolonged your dream, would you consider that damage? Where you are now is what you spoke about and if you are tired of being there, start speaking about something else.

Receive the gifts of grace and mercy.

You have been walking through life carrying dead weight and not enjoying your journey although you have always had the power within you to change. You lived beneath My plan for you and partied in your pity. You selfishly ruined your life for a season and just as you ruined it, you can fix it for your next season. Can your dream still live? Oh, yes it can!

Speak Life!

It is time to stop speaking out of your emotions and begin speaking My Word. I have not given you the spirit of fear but of love, power, and a sound mind (2 Timothy 1:7). Receive My gift and return to the devil what belongs to him, the spirit of fear. I have a good life planned for you. Do not abort it with the thoughts of the enemy. Remember, his plan is always to steal, kill, and destroy (John 10:10).

What did I say?

Lord, I breathe a sigh of relief because You said I can change my situation by speaking life. The thoughts and plans You have for me are good and not evil. It's not too late for me to ask for what I want, I only need to speak life and believe. I have been living beneath Your plan for my life and having a pity party about it. It's time for me to live the life Jesus came to give me.

Thoughts for you, the Reader...

What have you said regarding your dreams that may have prolonged the manifestation of them?

_____
_____
_____
_____
_____

What will you say now about your dreams and about your life?

_____
_____
_____
_____
_____

What will you do differently to insure your dreams manifest?

_____
_____
_____
_____
_____

Review the scriptures given for this day and record what God reveals to you.

Proverbs 18:21

2 Timothy 1:7

John 10:10

What are your thoughts regarding your dreams; what did you hear God say?

_____
_____
_____
_____
_____

Today's Prayer: *Thank You, Lord, for being so patient with me. Your Word has taught me that life and death are in the power of my tongue and that I can change my situation when I change my words. Forgive me for being so careless with my words, Lord, I truly repent. I realize my words were doing Satan's dirty work. No more will I work for him to sabotage my life and anyone else's. The power You have given me I will use responsibly as my desire is to please You!*

Today's Affirmation
(Say Aloud)

I am Powerful

I am a World Changer

I am Capable of. . .(fill in the blank)

Write Your Vision

I decree and declare from this moment forward I will _____

_____

_____

_____

_____

_____

_____

_____

_____

_____

_____

Clean Slate

Day 18
Starting Over

"Starting Over is to begin doing something again; to begin to happen again."

(Merriam-Webster Dictionary)

God is longsuffering (patient)! God is the master Creator (Genesis 1). There was purpose for everything made, including humans/mankind, however, because the heart of most were evil, so were their deeds. Everywhere God looked evil was prevalent, so He decided to start over with Noah's family after the flood (Genesis chapters 6 and 7). The rainbow in the sky is God's promise to never destroy all living creatures and the earth again with water (Genesis 9:8-17).

Have you ever had a plan for something or someone and saw that it wasn't going according to plan? In fact, it was getting worse so you said, "I need to start over." I have made that statement many times.

In my opinion, being a people pleaser is not a great personality trait, because people pleasers tend to attract in their lives those who are selfish, users, and manipulators. These people want what they want and will do and say anything to get their way even when it means destroying the lives of those who aim to please.

This used to be me in the worse way. In fact, regret is the meal I ate for years thinking about how I allowed myself to be mistreated. The dialogue that follows offers insight into my true experience.

My Regret!

Lord, I want to start over. I feel like I have made a mess of certain seasons of my life and I want a chance to start again. I spent so much time caring about what others think that I don't think of myself. Their thoughts of me are full of their own insecurities and lack of happiness, however, I let it be projected onto me. I have allowed negative treatment as if to say, "I don't think I'm better than you" or "See, I relate." How ridiculous! I let myself go down in what I consider the gutter because of that people pleasing trait. What person in his or her right mind goes from clean (not perfect) and happy in every area of their lives to dirty and sad to please another?

When you know better, do better.

Why does a confident person spend his or her days constantly listening to one who isn't? Only You can fix the broken, however, what happens is those who are broken won't come to You, they go to those who will listen with compassion seeking their next victim. They are strategic seeking whom they can devour while the once confident person with a heart to help is oblivious.

Getting what one wants is the name of the game no matter who gets hurt in the process. I think I didn't like myself too much to allow such mistreatment. Maybe I wasn't as confident as I thought or maybe I just had a weakness that was preyed upon by the predator and a heart that was easily manipulated.

Be balanced.

I find it difficult to believe that a person who allows his or herself to be controlled by another's opinion and actions just to be liked or loved does not have much love for who You created in them. I now know that You made us all different with unique personalities, gifts, and talents. When we allow who You created to be silenced because we want to fit in and not be misunderstood, that's the problem.

Don't look back!

Can I start over, Father? I need a chance to prove to myself what is love, respect, and admiration. I need to show myself that my life is worth living and enjoying. I need to give myself a chance to make amends with myself and run towards my potential and my possibilities. I did the wrong thing for all the wrong reasons; can I please have a do-over?

Love heals.

Let me say, I love myself again and now that I do, I clearly recognize the moments when I didn't. Thank You, Lord, for helping me get out of that dark and depressing season. I can boldly say and mean it when I do, "I love who I am, and I'm excited about who I am becoming."

Believe and Receive.

All things are possible to them that believe, including the ability to start over (Mark 9:23). What you need to do is capture that moment in time and repent. From the moment you do, begin to create what you feel you missed. If you did not live life to the fullest then, do it now. Feel the joy, laughter, and confidence you were supposed to feel. As you do that, you are giving yourself a double portion. You are being paid back with 100 percent interest all because you care enough to start again.

Live!

Do not lose your zeal for life. You owe it to yourself to be as spectacular as I created you to be. You owe yourself this feeling and the healing that comes with it. You owe it to yourself to be authentic and as real and powerful as I made you. People are watching. Show them how perseverance looks. Write your comeback story and live it well. Believe in the power you have been given and unlock some doors.

Get yourself to a place where your cup runs over, then help someone else.

They overcome when you speak.

Teach others that it is never too late and if there is a need to start over, it can be done. When you come across those who do not need to start over, encourage them to protect the precious gift of life they have been given and enjoy it. This is a life lesson you need to learn. Never take another moment for granted. Treat your life as the gift it is, giving thanks continuously. Be courageous and live life as it should be lived with adventure, reverence, thanksgiving, love, and so much more. I am come that you might have life and have it more abundantly (John 10:10).

What did I say?

God, what I heard You say is all things are possible when I believe (Mark 9:23). That means I can start over and so I will. It's not too late to live life to its fullest. You don't want me to lose my zeal for life. I owe it to myself to experience the best. I can teach others that it is never too late to be great. Life is full of lessons; I need to learn them and enjoy life's journey. My past is a part of my lesson and my future is my blessing! Lastly, You told me to spend my time with You and in doing so, I get all the validation I need. Thank You for being a God of a second chance.

Thoughts for you, the Reader. . .

If you answer yes to any of these questions, now is a good time to close the book on that part of your story and write another one. Don't let your past steal another moment of your present and future. Endure for your promise!

What times in your life do you wish you could do-over?

_____

_____

_____

_____

Are you living with regret or have you chosen to see them as life lessons to not only teach you, but perhaps someone coming behind you?

_____

_____

_____

_____

_____

What will you teach them?

How do you know you learned the lessons attached to your regrets?

Why do you think it's hard to let go of past mistakes?

How do you know you have totally forgiven yourself? How will you treat yourself going forward?

Review the scriptures given for this day and record what God reveals to you.

Genesis 1

Genesis 6 and 7

Starting Over

Genesis 9:8-17

Mark 9:23

John 10:10

Jeremiah 29:11

When you considering starting over, what did you hear God say?

_____

_____

_____

_____

Today's Prayer: *Thank You for teaching me about myself and reminding me that I am wonderfully made by Your mighty hand. I have made a bunch of mistakes being a people pleaser. Forgive me for putting people above You. That wasn't my intention. However, I realize most times when I people pleased I was allowing their voices to be louder than Yours. Thank You for being a second chance God and allowing me another opportunity to live a fantastic life, in Jesus' name I pray, Amen.*

Today's Affirmations

(Say Aloud)

I am Fearfully and Wonderfully made

I am a Masterpiece

I am Capable of. . .(fill in the blank)

Write Your Vision

I decree and declare from this moment forward I will _____

_____
_____
_____
_____
_____
_____
_____
_____
_____
_____

Day 19
No More Shrinking

"To shrink means to contract or curl up the body or part of it: huddle, cower; to lose substance; to lessen in value: dwindle; to recoil instinctively; to hold oneself back: refrain."

(Merriam-Webster Dictionary)

In the Bible, God's first encounter talking to Moses was through a burning bush (Exodus 3:1-17). Naturally, Moses was startled, however, when God began giving him instructions about the mission He needed him for, Moses began shrinking (vs.11) and making excuses. As you continue reading the story, you will see that although God was with and working through Moses, at times he didn't see himself as God saw him, which caused him to shrink.

I totally relate to the story of Moses in many ways. I know God has called me to do some great things for Him. However, because it's God's mission and it involves people, I never wanted to mislead and cause anyone to stumble. God believed in me more than I believed in myself. I didn't recognize God would be working through me. I felt like it was going to be all me and I became concerned with the opinion of people and began shrinking.

In my mind, when people do things for themselves it mainly affects them, but when people do things in the name of the Lord, it affects many. Although I am a good person with a good heart, my intention would not have been to hurt anyone, but people scrutinize until they find a reason and I wasn't mentally prepared, so I would shrink.

I finally realized there are more people for me and the need of what I possess was greater than the fear that once held me back, so I let it go. I became ready mentally, spiritually, emotionally, and physically. I wanted to be used of God and saw it as an honor that He would call me to serve. I got over myself quickly and repented. God spoke to me like only He can and straightened me out.

Stop shrinking!

I know why you shrink, you know why you shrink, and those who are in tuned with you know why you shrink. It is time for you to stop shrinking. Contrary to what you have been believing, your shrinking does not help, it hurts. I know it may be easier to navigate through life blending in, but when you were created to stand out, you can stand amid the crowd and still be seen.

I created you to soar!

It is such a lack of gratitude to see My children shrink beneath potential. The thief wishes and works consistently on you shrinking with hopes of you disappearing, being unseen and unheard. Do not give him what he wants. See yourself for who you are, the person I created you to be. Do you want your happily ever after, your abundance, your smile, your joy? Stop shrinking! You will never get to the good part of your life by shrinking.

Focus on you.

People may not like or understand you. You have experienced that already, it is no big deal. It will be the same when you get to where you want to go, so stop shrinking and check that off as knowledge learned. Those who want you to stay small are not for you even if you happen to call them friend or family. You must know when to let go so that you can grow.

Trust Me!

No longer put question marks where I put periods. Learn to accept what I allow and know that it will all work together for your good (Romans 8:28). Trust Me and trust My plan for your life. You can never let go of more than I give. Trust this process. I know what is best for you, so please listen.

Do you trust Me enough to listen, hear, and obey? Do you trust Me enough to step out and do the things I put in your heart to do? Do you trust Me enough to let go of your agenda? I want to see and feel trust from you!

Stop hiding!

No more of you being a best-kept secret, your voice matters. Your gifts, talents, and abilities were given on purpose. You are not a mistake! I do not make junk. Work what I have given you and grow where needed. Make no apologies for how I made you, only apologize for the ways of the world that you acquired that have taken you away from being your authentic self.

You matter!

Come back to Me and see yourself as you should, no more shrinking. When you truly see yourself, you will see possibilities, love, and purpose. Once you accept purpose, you live! "For I am come," says Jesus, "that you might have life and have it more abundantly" (John 10:10). Purpose causes abundant life and the joy of living. See yourself now and stop shrinking.

What did I say?

Father, You said it is time for me to live authentically. You have a great plan for my life that You want me to experience, however, shrinking keeps me far from it. It is time for me to stop shrinking. When I shrink for others, it shows a lack of gratitude for the way You created me. I must let go to grow and stop putting question marks where You have put periods. No more being the best-kept secret, my voice matters. I matter!

Thoughts for you, the Reader...

Embrace your greatness. If you have been shrinking so people can like you, news flash, they don't like you. I had to learn the same thing, so I am not being mean, just want you to know the truth. You were made for a purpose, so don't let the need to be liked by man/woman stop you from being used by God.

Shrinking is a trap used to hinder the progress of believers, what traps have you fallen in due to not being authentic?

_____

_____

_____

Shrinking is a form of being disobedience. What is within you (i.e. ideas, inventions, etc.) that has been trying to come out that you will not allow?

_____

_____

_____

What has God told you about yourself that makes you happy, yet, at times you find hard to believe?

_____

_____

_____

What will you do to assure what God has said about you comes to pass?

_____

_____

_____

Review the scriptures given for this day and record what God reveals to you.

Exodus 3:1-17

_____

_____

_____

Romans 8:28

_____

_____

_____

_____

_____

John 10:10

_____

_____

_____

_____

When you consider shrinking for whatever reason, what did you hear God say?

_____

_____

_____

_____

Today's Prayer: *Thank You, Father, for being so patient with me. I know I have not always done the things I should have done, please forgive me! You made me to stand out, but I have been blending in, for reasons that are so foolish. It will not happen again. I am not ashamed of who I am. I will proudly walk in my confidence and represent You well. Help me to always be authentically me, in Jesus' name, Amen.*

Today's Affirmations

(Say Aloud)

I am Phenomenal

I am Authentically Me

I am Capable of. . .(fill in the blank)

Write Your Vision

I decree and declare from this moment forward I will _____

_____

_____

_____

_____

_____

_____

_____

_____

_____

_____

Day 20
When You Know Better, Do Better!

"Better is to improve."
(Merriam-Webster Dictionary)

A great example of getting better is the story of Daniel and his friends. In Daniel 1:1-20, they were given certain delicacies to eat from the King's palace, but they did not want to defile themselves with that food. Daniel then asked for a specific diet for himself and the three Hebrew boys. This diet consisted of vegetables and water. The person in charge didn't want to honor his request, but he did for ten days. After the ten days were complete, they were examined and in everything were found to be ten times better.

We can all do better in areas of our lives. I know I can do better. It's a matter of making good choices. Sitting around feeling sorry for yourself is not a good choice and that's what I did for a season. While talking to God about it, He sure did set me straight, for as the Bible says in Proverbs 3:12, "for the Lord corrects those He loves (NLT)." Yes, He does.

Wake Up!

Stop sleeping on the job (life). Look at the time you have wasted. You have done enough spectating. It is time for you to start participating in your life and live. Your dreams are waiting to be realized and made into great manifestations. Do not keep talking about them; show us what you have seen so that we can enjoy it with you.

No more empty promises.

How long will you make us wait? Look around, I know you see the need. You can do better than you are doing, so, do better. There are cries for help all around you; in fact, the loudest cry is within you. I know you hear it because I do, yet you keep stalling and not allowing your gift to make room for you (Proverbs 18:16).

Use your gifts and talents!

When you put into action the thing that you know to do, your life will immediately get better. It happens because that one action will ignite a desire to do more; and as you continue being purpose driven, before you know it, you will have manifestation. Just as you see what has appeared from the workings of others, you will see yours, too.

Get Started!

Get up and get moving while you can, because the worse words you could utter about your dreams are "should have, would have, could have." We want to see you thrive, live, and be happy doing what you are called to do in this season of your life. Remember, old things are passed away, behold all thing are made new (2 Corinthians 5:17), that includes your old mindset and actions. They worked for you back then, but behold, it is time for the new. New thoughts, new ideas, new walk, new talk; you have a dream to realize and people are ready to see your good works and give Me glory (Matthew 5:16).

Let your light so shine!

How do you think most people get inspired? They get inspired when My children show up in the world shining their light. Their light causes them to see their way out of darkness and show them that possibilities really are possible. Faith comes by hearing the Word of God (Romans 10:17), yet for those who do not know how to use their faith, seeing the light in others, in most cases, is what reconciles them (their hearts) back to Me.

You are fearfully and wonderfully made.

I need you to want to be who you authentically are and not who you have become. When the world sees the real you, that will be the moment your light shines the brightest. Everyone, including Me, wants what is real. Take off the mask, peel back the layers, stop hiding behind the hurt, and be seen.

You are free to be you and whom the Son makes free is free indeed (John 8:36). Walk in your authenticity. You were born to manifest My goodness. When you fully embrace yourself, we all will see you being better in every area of your life.

What did I say?

Lord, You told me to wake up, stop stalling, and wasting time. It's time for me to be a doer of Your Word not just a hearer. Old things are passed away, which includes my old mindset and actions, it's time for the new to show up. When I put into action what I am called to do, my life will get better. People get inspired when I let my light shine. It's time for me to do better, because I know better.

Thoughts for you, the Reader...

There is nothing dull about you, for everything God made was good including you! It's time to stop being like everyone else and stand out, as you are a peculiar person chosen by God. Don't let imitating others and hiding your gift stop you from receiving your promises!

What gifts and talents do you have?

_____

_____

_____

_____

What do you plan to do with them?

_____

_____

_____

_____

Why were you afraid to use your gifts and abilities?

People are waiting for you to shine your light, what measures will you take to make sure we see it?

Review the scriptures given for this day and record what God reveals to you.

Proverbs 18:16

2 Corinthians 5:17

_____

_____

_____

_____

Matthew 5:16

_____

_____

_____

_____

Romans 10:17

_____

_____

_____

_____

When you consider doing better, what did you hear God say?

_____

_____

_____

_____

Today's Prayer: *Thank You, Father God, for having mercy on me. I do know that I can do better than I am doing, please forgive me for sitting on my gift. I will use my gifts and talents to increase Your kingdom and will not allow others' opinions of my gifts stop me. You make no mistakes and You made me in a way that pleases You, so thank You. I will fulfill the purpose and calling You have for my life.*

Today's Affirmations

(Say Aloud)

I am Spectacular

I am Extraordinary

I am Capable of. . .(fill in the blank)

Write Your Vision

I decree and declare from this moment forward I will _____

_____

_____

_____

_____

_____

_____

_____

_____

_____

_____

Life Lesson

Day 21
The Struggle Within

> "Good - of a favorable character or tendency;
> Bad – failing to reach an acceptable standard."
> *(Merriam-Webster Dictionary)*

There are so many examples of being both good and bad. The Bible is full of people who had these tendencies. Consider King Saul, who was a good king for a season of his life until he became bad by disobeying God and doing things his way (1 Samuel 13–1 Samuel 15).

King David had experiences with good and bad as well. He was a man after God's own heart (Acts 13:22), then he committed adultery (2 Samuel 11) and tried to cover it up, which lead to murder. There are so many people I could bring to the forefront, but when you read the Scriptures, the picture becomes clearer.

As much as I try and have tried to do everything right, there have been times I have fallen short. I believe this happens for several reasons; one, as previously stated, no one is perfect, and two, because I desperately need Jesus. In the thoughts that follow, you will read a conversation I had with God regarding my concerns with my good and bad thoughts, words, and actions. Hopefully, you will read something that will help you along your journey. Enjoy.

Everyone makes mistakes.

Father, why does it seem like bad thoughts and words manifest fast and good thoughts and words manifest slow? It makes me so sad just thinking about the crazy thoughts that have gone through my mind as well as the words that have come out of my mouth. Help me! What must I do to change the outcome?

Who or what is controlling your thoughts?

It is because you believe the negative or bad thoughts and words when you only want the good thoughts and words. You put more faith in the negative coming to pass/manifesting than you do the positive. You put faith and fear into the bad, and all those emotions are firing in the same direction, so of course, something will be hit.

Nothing is too hard for Me!

Change your mind, your words, and your actions, and you will truly live the life you want to live. I am your heavenly Father and I love you too much to let you stay in the negative state of being for which your mind and words have placed you. Trust Me and truly believe that I can do exceedingly, abundantly, above all you can ask or think (Ephesians 3:20) and I do it all according to your faith and belief. Do you believe? You are more than a conqueror through Christ and it is time for you to show up in your life. You have allowed your mind and actions to cause you to experience the worse; Stop It! Change your mind and change your life.

I AM that I AM!

I am God, the creator of the universe. You were made in My image. No more of this barely getting by, barely making it mentality. You were created to thrive. Tell yourself what you were created to do and your mind will listen. You were created to win and make manifest the things of God. You were created to make a positive difference and show others how to do the same just by watching your life. You were created to heal and walk in health, to teach and train, to give, to love, and from some things, abstain. You were created for greatness. Go, create and be great.

What did I say?

Lord, You said the manifestation of my negative thoughts and actions can be a thing of the past when I speak life over my life. You said I put faith in negative things coming to pass and that's why I have experienced negative. I need to trust and believe that You can do exceedingly, abundantly above all I can ask or think. You are the creator of the universe and You created me to thrive. You told me to tell myself what I was created to do and my mind will listen. I am created for greatness.

Thoughts for you, the Reader...

If you have been speaking and pondering negative thoughts and words, now is a good time to let them go. You are better than the negativity that desires to sift joy from your life. It's time to stand up and live your life like you have been set apart for something amazing.

What negative thoughts do you ponder?
_____
_____
_____
_____

What negative relationships are you still holding on to, why?
_____
_____
_____
_____
_____

What has manifested in your life because of your negative thoughts and actions?

_____
_____
_____
_____

What will you do to counter attack the negative thoughts that come to your mind?

_____
_____
_____
_____

Review the scriptures given for this day and record what God reveals to you.

1 Samuel 13–1 Samuel 15

_____
_____
_____
_____

The Struggle Within

Acts 13:22

2 Samuel 11

Matthew 19:26

Ephesians 3:20

When you consider your inner struggle(s), what did you hear God say?

_____

_____

_____

_____

Today's Prayer: *Thank You, Lord, for giving me the revelation of believing and just wanting. I understand now and I know that I must believe to receive. I know Your Word says in (Hebrews 11:6), without faith it is impossible to please You and faith is believing. I believe!*

The Struggle Within

Today's Affirmations

(Say Aloud)

I am Good

I am Aligned with the will of God

I am Capable of. . .(fill in the blank)

Write Your Vision

I decree and declare from this moment forward I will _____

_____
_____
_____
_____
_____
_____
_____
_____
_____
_____
_____

Never Forget

Day 22
Remember

"Remember is to bring to mind or think of again."
(Merriam-Dictionary)

When I think of the word remember, the story in the Bible that comes to mind is that of the prodigal son (Luke 15:11-32). He had everything he needed at home but wasn't happy, so he asked his father for the portion of his inheritance that he would receive. He took his money, possessions, went far away, and began to live a riotous life. Then something happened and he remembered. Upon remembering, he decided to humble himself before his father and go back home. His father received him without question and with open arms. It's an amazing story of forgiveness that you must read.

In my life, I recall times when I had to remember who I was and who truly loved me. Life can be like a rollercoaster, with dips, swings, jerks, bumps, and harsh stops. I must admit, during those times I wasn't always sure that God loved me and honestly, my actions didn't show that I loved myself. Thank God for the ability to believe again. I had to remember what was true and that's the love of God. His love is unmatched, incomparable, and indescribable. God loves me and He loves you, too. Never forget how much you are loved.

Always remember!

Remember who you are by remembering Whose you are, a child of the Most High God. You belong to Me! Pretending to be someone you are not hurts you and those attached to you. I have need of you; there are people you need to meet and places you need to go. Not embracing who I made you to be prolongs your progress. I am God and I made no mistake with you. You can behave better than what I have seen, look deep within yourself and remember.

Remember the times when you spoke with such confidence and boldness. Remember how your life was during those times; the happiness you experienced, the joy you felt, the great things manifested. You can have that again and so much more if you can imagine a better life and work to obtain it.

I miss you!

Sometimes, I look at where you are and say, today will be the day to remember My voice and how we used to communicate. Today will be the day when you remember My Word is where you found the solution to all your problems. Today, you will remember our relationship. I want that back and I know you want it, too. You want and need it, so remember.

Feelings can change.

Father, I feel wrong inside. I feel like I have caused so much unnecessary trauma in my life; so much I've had to experience because I forgot about myself. I spoke death instead of life. I allowed the cares I had to be close to me instead of casting them to Jesus (1 Peter 5:7). It saddens me to think of how my life might have been without the negative and damaging self-talk. I would say things about myself and later would voice, "What did I just say?" I know that death and life are in the power of the tongue (Proverbs 18:21), and it's important to speak life, so when I didn't, I immediately became frightened because of the possible negative fruit that could have appeared.

It was a crazy time. I felt so much fear, worry, and doubt. It's like I no longer believed, but deep inside I did. At times, it was like I was looking at myself and seeing someone else, listening to myself and hearing someone else. The battle in my mind was real. I felt alone and in the dark and it seemed every time I tried to get some light or peace, I was pulled back and surrounded further by darkness. It was scary. I couldn't focus on good things as it says in Your Word. Every time I would think of something good, something negative would quickly enter my mind. It was the most challenging mental moment of my life.

Remember the mission of the thief.

The devil comes to steal, kill, and destroy (John 10:10), and although he succeeded in his mission against you for years, he hasn't won. I will make him pay for all he caused in your life and give you double for your troubles. Your life is not over, I know how to redeem the time. He planted seeds of allusions and lies causing you to fear, but what the enemy did not realize is you called on the name of Jesus and received help. I am here to remind you what the scripture says in 1 Corinthians 2:9, "No eye has seen, no ear has heard, and no mind has imagined what God has prepared for those who love Him" (NLT).

I know how to give beauty for ashes (Isaiah 61:3) and will never let the enemy win when it comes to you. You will have the last laugh and your tears of sadness will turn into tears of joy. Instead of shame and dishonor, you will enjoy a double share of honor. You will possess a double portion of prosperity in your land and everlasting joy will be yours (Isaiah 61:7). Nothing you have gone through is lost, I can turn your mess into a miracle and make it your message. You will soon be able to say to your enemy, "You intended to harm me, but God intended it all for good. He brought me to this position, so I could save the lives of many people (Genesis 50:20 NLT).

The race is given to those who endure to the end.

This past season was a challenge, but you made it through. You woke up and remembered! You remembered who I am.

You turned the pages of the Bible and became encouraged. You read that you could speak to any mountain in your life and tell it to go away (Mark 11:23) and that all things are possible when you believe (Mark 9:23). You have been given keys to the Kingdom of Heaven and the authority to give your problems, circumstances, and situations an expiration date (Mark 11:12-23). You had to go through some things, but you did not give up, instead, you are enduring for your promise and enduring until the end.

What did I say?

Father, what I heard You say is Your Word is full of wonderful promises that speak of a marvelous life for me. You told me not to believe the lies from the enemy. He has been working tirelessly to accomplish his mission in my life. You told me not to worry because You know how to redeem the time and give me beauty for ashes. You know how to give me a double share of honor for my shame. I am still here for a reason and if I continue and endure for my promise, I will obtain it. Lord, I shall always remember.

Remember

Thoughts for you, the Reader...

Always remember who you are and walk in your God-given authority. Remember who created you, who blessed you with gifts, talents, and ability and who loves you, unconditionally. Don't let the lies from the enemy stop you from being your best.

Which moment in your life marks the time when your actions showed you needed to remember?

_____

_____

_____

_____

Who in your life has helped to remind you of your purpose?

_____

_____

_____

_____

What will you do from this moment on to protect your God given promises?

___

Review the scriptures given for this day and record what God reveals to you.

Luke 15:11-32

___

1 Peter 5:7

___

Proverbs 18:21

Remember

John 10:10

1 Corinthians 2:9

Isaiah 61:3

Isaiah 61:7

Genesis 50:20

Mark 11:23

Mark 9:23

Mark 11:12-23

Remember

When you consider what you need to remember, what did you hear God say?

_____

_____

_____

_____

Today's Prayer: *Thank You, Lord, for Your lovingkindness towards me. You are an amazing Father, who loves unconditionally. I have such hope now and it's all because of You! I appreciate You and will always remember who I am, a child of the Creator of the universe. You, Father, are the one who makes no mistakes.*

Today's Affirmations

(Say Aloud)

I am Blessed

I am One of a Kind

I am Capable of. . .(fill in the blank)

Write Your Vision

I decree and declare from this moment forward I will _____

_____

_____

_____

_____

_____

_____

_____

_____

_____

Day 23
Don't Let Your Mind Kill You

Mind (Greek: nous) – Your inner self that feels and thinks and is created to tune into the mind of Christ.
(1 Corinthians 2:16)

The United Negro College Fund has a slogan that reads, "A Mind is a Terrible Thing to Waste." Although their slogan focuses on education, we waste our minds when we think negatively. Our minds have creative power so to create negative things when you can create things that are positive in my opinion is wasting your mind.

There was a season in my life when it seemed as if I could not think straight. When I wanted to think positive, negative thoughts would quickly enter. At one point it seemed uncontrollable. It was a scary time and I would think to myself, my mind is against me.

I had to do a lot of praying, fasting, and reading to get my mind thinking as it should. God is patient. He showed me what I needed to do and what I needed to stop doing to have the results I desired. He reminded me that I needed to have a mind like Christ (Philippians 2:5) and to let go of my sabotaging mind. There is power in positive thinking. When God talks I listen, now it's your turn. . .

Think on these things. . .

Your mind is powerful. It plays a vitally important part in your life, so you must guard it from unwanted intruders. There is a real enemy seeking to destroy you and the place he headquarters is in the mind. The thoughts that tear down the core of who you are, are not from Me. I sent Jesus because of love. Jesus came that you might have an abundant life (John 10:10). Thoughts that come against you experiencing abundant life are not from Me.

Pictures do not lie.

Your facial expressions are indicators of your thoughts, for they tell the story of happiness, sadness, anger, worry, etc. Sometimes, you can tell the general category a person is in with regards to their thoughts just by looking at them. Think about it. How many times can you recall asking someone what is on their mind or if they are okay just because of the way they looked? The mind is powerful and that is why I implore you to use it for good and not allow it to be used for evil.

Your thoughts matter!

Think about what you spend most of your time thinking about. There is a plan for your life (John 10:10) and your thoughts about yourself are driving you closer to your God-given plan or that of the devil. Examine your life for a moment, and for this example compartmentalize yourself. In your friendships, have your thoughts brought you closer or caused division? In your family, what have thoughts caused you to do? Think of other areas of your life, is there more stealing, killing, and destroying going on or is there abundant life? Even if you are somewhere in the middle, it is not My best for you so think differently.

Think on things that are praiseworthy.

Thoughts that you ponder can make you sick as well as the ability to make you well. At any given moment, you can change your life and make it better than it is. You must want better, believe that you deserve better, ask Me for better, and think better. At any given moment you change your mind and you can change your life. Your life can be better when you think on things that matter (Philippians 4:8). Don't let your mind kill you! Speak life!

Speak the Word only!

Speak truth to every lie whispered and once you speak it, get on it. If your thoughts are suggesting sadness, declare "the joy of the Lord is my strength" (Nehemiah 8:9) and do something that makes you happy. If your thoughts are suggesting sickness, declare "by His stripes I am healed" (Isaiah 53:5) and begin to act like you are healed while thanking Me for restoring your body to wholeness. If thoughts are suggesting death, declare "I will live and not die and declare the works of the Lord" (Psalm 118:17). If your thoughts are suggesting that you are not loved, declare "for God loved me so much He sent Jesus" and because of Jesus I can have the best life (John 3:16).

Speak life and live!

Tell your mind about My promises to you. Submerge it with the goodness and grace of My words. Allow your mind to experience a tsunami of good, so much so that the negative suffocates and is no more. Imagine what that looks and feels like and see yourself there experiencing it now. Tell your mind what you expect and prepare yourself to receive it. Do not let your mind kill you. Think on things that make you smile, be happy, and feel right.

Love your life!

It feels right to live an abundant life, so think about it. It feels right to be healthy and whole, so think about it. It feels right to laugh loud, so think about the things that make you laugh. It feels right to see your situation turn around for good. See it better and see yourself higher. It is time to live, so do not let your mind kill you.

When you change, things will change!

When will you take your leap of faith? Do not let your mind kill you, make it bless you! Make up your mind and get settled once and for all and do good. Let the world know who you are and stop hiding. Stop hiding behind your past mistakes and stop listening to the lies that are spoken. You are forgiven. Stop hiding behind doubt and fear and stop hiding behind your lack of money. I can supply all your needs (Philippians 4:19). Stop hiding.

Make your mind work for you.

Think on the things that will cause your greatest joy, and when you accomplish what you thought about, think on more. As you meditate on the things of God, the fruit of joy will grow abundantly in you. Make a habit to starve the negative thoughts and feed the positive ones. Your life truly does depend on it. Do not just make it a habit for a period in your life; make it a lifestyle. When it becomes a lifestyle, people will admire your good works and give all praises, honor, and glory to Me (Matthew 5:16).

Think on things that matter!

Your good thoughts not only help you, they help the world. Good thoughts precede good actions and good actions are contagious. No matter the negative we see in the world, good outweighs it. Once good finds its place, great will ensue. Since you are now knowledgeable about the power of your mind, use it for good and become great. Be the person you have always wanted to be. Remember your young mind before the contamination? What did you utter out of your mouth? Think back to the first time someone asked you what you wanted to become when you grew up. That was an innocent time with pure thoughts. What did you say before someone told you why you could not be it?

You are chosen for greatness!

Find that younger you and go after that dream. It is not too late. Your time has not passed. Go for it. True, there are those who knew who they wanted to become when they were younger and became it, but there are also those who realized or remembered later in life and still became it. It is not too late.

Stop daydreaming and live. Make your mind up. Let it heal and not kill you. Think on these things. . .(Philippians 4:8).

What did I say?

Lord, what I heard You say is that my mind is powerful and that I have the power and ability to guard it. I must think on things that are good and not focus on the bad. My life will change when my mind changes. I can speak life to every lie spoken to me. It's time for me to take a leap of faith. You told me to tell my mind of Your goodness and submerge it with Your promises to me. I am to tell my mind what I expect and prepare to receive it. I must remember my young mind and the endless possibilities it conceived before the contaminations from life and believe again.

Thoughts for you, the Reader...

Let go of what no longer matters. It's time for you to grow to another level so you must learn to control your mind. Think on things that make you happy, things you want to see manifest, and leave the rest behind.

What is the dominate thought that drives you?

_____

_____

_____

_____

Discuss the direction your thought has you going and is it making you smile or frown?

_____

_____

_____

_____

What's on your mind now?

_____
_____
_____
_____

Now that truth is revealed, what will you do when you think of negative thoughts?

_____
_____
_____
_____

Review the scriptures given for this day and record what God reveals to you.

Philippians 2:5

_____
_____
_____
_____

John 10:10

Philippians 4:8

Nehemiah 8:9

Isaiah 53:5

Psalm 118:17

John 3:16

Philippians 4:19

Matthew 5:16

Philippians 4:8

When you consider the power of your mind, what did you hear God say?

Today's Prayer: *Thank You, Father, for teaching me on the power of the mind. I now know how powerful it really is and that I need to focus and work hard to keep it renewed. Thank You for being so gracious and patient with me. I no longer allow my mind to take me on a trip, I think on things that are pure in Jesus' name.*

Today's Affirmations

(Say Aloud)

I am an Independent Thinker

I am Focused

I am Capable of. . .(fill in the blank)

Write Your Vision

I decree and declare from this moment forward I will _____

_____

_____

_____

_____

_____

_____

_____

_____

_____

_____

_____

Day 24
Created to...

"The root word of created is create which means to bring into existence; to produce or bring about by a course of action or behavior, through imaginative skill."
(Merriam-Webster Dictionary)

God is Creator of Heaven and earth. He spoke the world into existence, saw what He said, looked at it all, and said, "It is very good" (Genesis 1). We are a part of the "very good" He saw, for when He created us, He made us in His image. Our God is an awesome God, He is the Master Creator.

When I think about being made in the image of God, I smile, blush, and say, *Thank You.* What a loving Father He is to make sure His children are equipped with the necessities of this life. I am aware of God's awesomeness, however, at times, I wasn't aware of mine. As I sat and listened to our Heavenly Father talk, I became encouraged again to do what He has done, and that is to walk in my authority and create. Now, it's your turn, be encouraged.

Created to...

I created you to stand out and oftentimes I see you blending in. Stand Out.

I created you to positively impact the world with your gifts, talents, and abilities. Are you doing it?

I asked you to love like I love without conditions, yet when I look at you and listen to your words, I am aware of the lack of love you possess.

I created you to forgive and you refuse. You find it right or justifiable holding people captive for their mistakes. You think it is good making them pay for your disappointment, yet what you have forgotten is if you hold on to their mistakes, I will hold on to yours (Matthew 6:14). If you do not truly forgive, you will not be forgiven and no one and nothing is worth Me not forgiving you for all the many things you do, have done, and will do. Forgive! Do not think about it, obey and do it, you are worth it.

I created you to soar like an eagle and no matter how I entice you with greatness, you choose to hang with chickens.

I created you to live an abundant life, yet a lot of what I hear from you is begging, as if you do not have any options or access to what you need.

I created you in My image, and when I look at you, there are times I see someone who has forgotten who they are and whose they are. Remember Me!

Remember Me and then remember you and begin making the adjustments to become authentically you. You and I both know you will never be as happy as your heart desires being like someone else. I made you special. Thank Me for creating you and begin treating yourself special. A beautiful handcrafted gift to the world is what I created when I made you. Embrace you!

I created you to increase My kingdom by reconciling those back to Me who have turned away and are lost. You do this by being a minister of reconciliation, which is one who will let his or her light and life shine so bright that people will ask, "What must I do to be saved?" (Acts 16:30).

I created you with the ability to break free from bondage and help free others. You have the authority in your mouth, use it and stay free.

You have been created to stop what has started and start what has stopped. You have been given the keys to the kingdom and whatever you bind on earth will be bound in Heaven and whatever you loose on earth shall be loosed in Heaven (Matthew 18:18). Use your authority!

You were created to get up after every fall; remember staying down excites the devil and getting up excites Me. Do not stop in failures, rise to victories! Mistakes are a part of life that keep you humble and remind you that no one on earth is perfect.

You were created to create, so make it good!

Created to...

Thoughts for you, the Reader...

What has God told you to create? Embrace your creativity.

_____
_____
_____
_____

Review the scriptures given for this day and record what God reveals to you.

Genesis 1

_____
_____
_____
_____

Matthew 6:14

_____
_____
_____
_____

Acts 16:30

Matthew 18:18

Today's Prayer: *Thank You, Father God, for the gifts and talents you have given me. I believe You have a great plan for my life. You created me to do great things and I will no longer sit and stare at the world. I will not waste any more precious moments, please forgive me. I will rise up and be great, in Jesus' name, Amen.*

Created to...

Today's Affirmations

(Say Aloud)

I am Creative

I am Bold

I am Capable of...(fill in the blank)

Write Your Vision

I decree and declare from this moment forward I will _____

_____

_____

_____

_____

_____

_____

_____

_____

_____

_____

Day 25
Next in Line

"*Immediately adjacent (as in place, rank or time)."*
(Merriam-Webster Dictionary)

God is fair. He will fulfill His promises. You never have to worry about God not doing what He said He would do for you because He cannot lie (Numbers 23:19).

How do you wait in line? Be honest. Do you grumble or are you patient and full of understanding? This is probably an unfair question because at times we all can probably say we do both depending on the situation and circumstance. The bottom line is God has a blessing with our names on it. I am ready for mine, are you?

You are a Prime Candidate!

You are a prime candidate for a miracle! The things you have been through were not for naught. Look at my servant Job. The devil asked for him and I allowed it. Then I gave him double for his trouble (Job 1). Consider your circumstances.

Think it not strange the length of trouble you endured while being faithful. It was full of purpose. Think it not strange that friends turned their back on you when you needed them most and think it not strange not hearing Me for a while. It was all because you are next in line for your miracle.

Be still and know that I am God!

My reasons for being quiet vary and none of them are because I do not care. Quite the opposite. My love for you runs so deep it is immeasurable. Your wildest dreams cannot take you to the place of My love for you. So, never let your lack of understanding convince you otherwise, I am love and I love you!

You are fearfully and wonderfully made.

The enemy knows how special you are and the gifts and talents that I gave you to increase the kingdom. He also knows the power you have and therefore, works tirelessly to oppress you. It has been like that from the beginning, yet you are still holding on. You are holding on to the promises I made you, knowing they are "Yes" and "Amen" (2 Corinthians 1:20). You are holding on to the faith I gave you to believe in what is not yet been seen. You are holding on to the victory I said was yours, and because you are yet holding on, you are next in line for your miracle.

I will never leave you nor forsake you.

I will not apologize for allowing you to go through what you have experienced. Who better to give the testimony that is 100 percent yours? Who else could have gone through what you went through with the grace and integrity you had? You made it through. I made sure you did and you are not coming out empty handed. David said, "It was good that I was afflicted" (Psalm 119:71). Although right now you may not feel the same as he did, look at the person you have become. Before, you would not pray for those who mistreat you, now look at you; I hear you praying for your enemies all the time now. This character trait and so many others are a result of your experiences and lessons learned along the way. I love you and stopped by to say, "Continue to wait, you are next in line."

What did I say?

Father, what I heard You say is, the things I have been through were not for nothing. I am next in line for a miracle. You love me and just because I didn't hear You from time to time doesn't mean You were not near. The enemy knows how special I am, and he works overtime to oppress and keep me from using my gifts. You told me to be watchful, and not to let him. You gave me examples of those You chose to go through negative things, and afterward, they were blessed twice as much as before. I, too, will receive my double portion blessing in Jesus' name.

Thoughts for you, the Reader...

God can do it for you. He can give you what you need to be whole in every area of your life. Don't stop asking, don't stop believing, and remember to have an attitude of gratitude while you wait. The Bible tells us in (Mark 11:23), when you pray, believe that you receive and you will have it. What you are expecting is expecting you, so keep believing and prepare for your testimony.

Consider the following questions:

For what are you believing to receive from God?

_____
_____
_____

Are there any instructions you've been given to receive your miracle? If so, what are they and are you doing them?

_____
_____
_____

Review the scripture given for this day and record the God-given revelation.

Numbers 23:19

_____
_____
_____
_____

Job 1

_____
_____
_____
_____

2 Corinthians 1:20

_____
_____
_____
_____

Next in Line

Psalm 119:71

Mark 11:23

When you consider being next in line, what did you hear God say?

Today's Prayer: *Thank You, Lord, for reminding me that delay does not mean denial. What You have for me is for me and I fully expect to receive it. I realize not reading Your Word is a trap set to keep me from knowledge and Your goodness. Forgive me, Father. I will feast on Your Word, (bread of life) and be full. I no longer walk in doubt and I let go of fear in the name of Jesus!*

Today's Affirmations

(Say Aloud)

I am Blessed.

I am Excited.

I am Capable of...(fill in the blank)

Write Your Vision

I decree and declare from this moment forward I will _____

_____
_____
_____
_____
_____
_____
_____
_____
_____
_____
_____

Restored

Day 26
Be Healed

"To heal means to make free from injury or disease; to make sound or whole; to make well again (restore to health); to cause (an undesirable condition) to be overcome (mend); to restore to original purity or integrity."
(Merriam-Webster Dictionary)

You can be healed of everything. Ephesians 3:20 says, "God is able to do exceeding abundantly above all you can ask or think according to the power that works in you." Your faith can move mountains even if that mountain is a need for healing. As you continue in your reading, put your faith to work overtime and get the healing you want. God has the answer to everything!

There are so many ways to be healed and live in health and wholeness, with each way having faith and belief as the core ingredient and foundation. There are so many miracles in the Bible, yet the one I want to focus on and talk about is the woman with the issue of blood (Mark 5:25-35).

What Did I Say?

Everyone has a story.

Imagine with me if you will, losing something that was vitally important to live life abundantly. Imagine not being able to stop the flow of blood for twelve years and becoming weaker and more frustrated as days go by. Becoming so desperate that you use all your resources to get the healing that seems to be nonexistent by all accounts known to man. "Nothing is working," you say to yourself, and now fear, doubt, worry, and thoughts of giving up have entered your mind and caused you to speak the most ungodly and damaging words one could say.

Faith moves mountains.

"Now what?" you wonder. What must happen to reverse the current flow of negative manifestation? For this woman, she heard about Jesus and the many miracles He performed and she believed. This woman believed if she could just touch a piece of His clothing, she would be made whole. This woman believed Jesus was the answer. The one who could not only stop the negative current flow she was experiencing but could instantly heal and restore every part of her that needed it. She believed! She had the faith to see her desire manifested, so much so, that she pressed her way through the crowd, stretched out her hand, reached, grabbed, and was healed.

What do you believe about Jesus?

Jesus is the way, the truth, and life (John 14:6). She believed those words. Do you? Jesus is love and our belief in Him connects us to His love. Jesus' love empowers us, it gives us peace, joy, strength, and it heals. Do you know that Jesus loves you? Do you believe you can be healed and restored? Do you believe you can live the rest of your life healed, whole, and happy?

Believe and Receive!

Healing is available for all who desire and believe. Miracles did not stop at the Bible, they happen every day for those who believe. Your life is a miracle! You must believe and have faith that good will change the result of what is bad, and the bad in your life only came to show you your power. You can be well my child if you want it. You must speak it and believe you deserve it and you can have it. You must want it enough that you see yourself in it, whatever it is; believe that all things are possible (Matthew 19:26) and they will be to you.

What did I say?

Father, You said healing is available to me, just as it was available to those of old. You are the same God and You still have power to heal. You said we must believe. I do believe, please help the areas of my unbelief.

Thoughts for you, the Reader...

If you have faith the size of a mustard seed you can speak to any mountain and tell it to be removed (Mark 11:23). The need for healing is a mountain.

Where are you on the path to belief?

_____

_____

_____

What is vitally important to you that seems to be running out and from you causing you to lose hope?

_____

_____

_____

What things are you seeking healing for?

_____

_____

_____

What Did I Say?

What words of faith are you speaking?

_____
_____
_____
_____

What declaration of God's Word supports your belief?

_____
_____
_____
_____

Review the scriptures given for this day and record what God reveals to you.

Ephesians 3:20

_____
_____
_____
_____

Mark 5:25-35

_____
_____
_____
_____

John 14:6

Matthew 19:26

Mark 11:23

When you consider being healed, what did you hear God say?

Today's Prayer: *Thank You, Father, for loving me so much that You sent Your Son Jesus to go through so much for me. I realize I don't have to be sick and I can be well if I believe and am bold enough to ask as it says in Matthew 7:7. I believe and I receive in Jesus' name, Amen!*

Today's Affirmations

(Say Aloud)

I am Healed

I am Healthy and Whole

I am Capable of. . .(fill in the blank)

Write Your Vision

I decree and declare from this moment forward I will _____

_____
_____
_____
_____
_____
_____
_____
_____
_____
_____

Day 27
The Blood of Jesus!

What can wash away your sins and make you whole again? Nothing but the blood of Jesus!

Jesus spilled His blood for you to live a powerful and blessed life, so live it as He intended.

Nothing can penetrate or come against the blood of Jesus, so plead the blood over everything that matters to you.

What does the blood of Jesus mean to you?

_____
_____
_____
_____

Today's Prayer: *Thank You for Jesus. I appreciate Him and all that He has done for me. I confess and believe that Jesus died for my sins, You raised Him from the dead, and now He sits on Your right side praying for me. I believe the blood of Jesus is powerful and can do anything. I am grateful for the blood of Jesus!*

The Blood of Jesus!

Today's Affirmations
(Say Aloud)

I am Covered by the blood of Jesus

I am Forgiven because of the blood of Jesus

I am Capable of. . .(fill in the blank)

Write Your Vision

I decree and declare from this moment forward I will

_____

_____

_____

_____

_____

_____

_____

_____

_____

_____

Day 28
Create Your Own Legacy

"A legacy is a gift by will especially money or other personal property; something transmitted by or received from an ancestor or predecessor or from the past."

(Merriam-Webster Dictionary)

I must admit, sometimes I look at what others have done and say, "Wow!" I admire and at times want to do the same, but how can I when I am not those I watch, I am me. This is the point God made to me when I was watching and daydreaming.

God is so kind. He knows how to gently get us back to ourselves. Life's journey is amazing to me. You never know where you may end up and what you may be doing. The thoughts, the actions, and the encounters are really amazing. Below you will read what God spoke to me about legacy. Hopefully, you will be blessed by it and receive something you can take away for yourself. Enjoy.

Let theirs go.

I know you wish you could be like them, but you cannot! You cannot have what they have, go where they go, do what they do, or leave what they have left or are leaving. Thou shalt not covet.

My plans for you are good.

I do not make mistakes. You are not a mistake nor is the creativity I put in you, so use it and create your own legacy. There is no wrong or right; there is only you and yours. What will it be?

What is authentically you?

Where is your passion? What drives you or makes your heart beat fast with excitement? What do you do the most, I mean every day or nearly daily that satisfies your soul? Who are you spending most of your time with and why? What about them makes you so happy and content?

You are created by and with the best.

I made you perfectly in My image, that means there is a part of you that is Me. Do you know what it is? Think about Me for a moment and think about the attributes that are Me. Describe Me as you know Me. Speak out loud, maybe even write My characteristics down so that you can see them and then do the same for yourself. Are there any similarities? Really think before you answer. Now tell Me what they are and remind yourself of the power within.

There is nothing missing, nothing lacking.

I purposefully created you with everything you need to live the most successful life imaginable, so do your part in this collaboration. Stop wanting to be like someone else and start wanting to be like the person I created you to be. Fall in love with yourself again. Remember that time when you absolutely loved being you? Remember the words you used to say when you looked in the mirror or at yourself in person or in pictures? Remember that feeling? You can have it again if you want it.

I love you!

The moment you shift your attention from what they are doing to what you can do, that feeling will resurface. There is no magic trick involved. It is simply making up your mind to give "you" a chance at a great life and legacy because you deserve it. I did not make you to be a copycat, I made you special.

Be authentic!

I have a great plan for your life and want to give you an expected end (Jeremiah 29:11). What are you expecting? Get with Me and learn My ways of doing things, so that you can have the life of your dreams. You cannot do it on your own. You can initiate, but getting to the finish line is going to take help.

My sheep know My voice.

I have the help you need. Do not be fooled by what is happening all around you. Know the truth and it will make you free (John 8:32). Guard your heart, watch your mouth, and do not believe everything you hear. My plan for you is good; the enemy's plan for you is bad, so do not believe the hype, know the counterfeits. Your legacy is worth leaving, create your own and let theirs go!

What did I say?

Father, what I heard You say is "be me." You didn't make a mistake creating me so there is no need to act like anyone else. I need to find my passion. You have already given me everything I need to live a great life. I need to shift my attention from what they are doing to what I can do and start doing it. I am full of purpose, I need to hear Your voice and I need to follow.

Thoughts for you, the Reader. . .

You can create your own legacy. You must let go of the tendency to be like another and embrace your own creativity. The plan that God has for you is great, so to focus on another is doing yourself a disservice. Don't let envy get in the way of what God has for you.

What do you know for sure that God wants for you?

_____
_____
_____
_____

What do you know for sure to be your God given gifts, talents, and abilities?

_____
_____
_____
_____

What will you do to achieve your success using your gifts, talents, and abilities?

_____
_____
_____
_____
_____

Review the scriptures given for this day and record what God reveals to you.

Jeremiah 29:11

_____
_____
_____
_____

John 8:32

_____
_____
_____
_____

What Did I Say?

When you consider your legacy, what did you hear God say?

_____
_____
_____
_____
_____

Today's Prayer: *Thank You, Lord for reminding me that the gifts and talents You gave to all Your children are important. No one is better than the other, for you love us all equally. Forgive me for focusing on other's gifts and talents and not working on my own. I know there is greatness in me, because I was created in Your image. I will do better and use my gifts, talents, and abilities to bless the world, in Jesus' name, Amen.*

Today's Affirmations

(Say Aloud)

I am Valuable

I am Gifted

I am Capable of. . .(fill in the blank)

Write Your Vision

I decree and declare from this moment forward I will _____

_____
_____
_____
_____
_____
_____
_____
_____
_____
_____

Day 29
If You Just Believe

"To believe is to consider to be true or honest; to accept the word or evidence of; to hold as an opinion."

(Merriam-Webster Dictionary)

God believes! God knows what He put in each one of us and knows what we can do. He doesn't worry about a thing; His faith is in His Word and in His own ability. Hebrews 6:13 says that when it comes to swearing by someone, since there is no one greater, He swears by Himself.

There was a time when God said to me, "If I can but believe, all things are possible" (Mark 9:23). Imagine the all in that scripture, there are no limits in all, in fact, the only limit is what I put out there. God is limitless and when I learn to trust Him with my entire life, not just pieces of it, He will cause it to be great. I trust God! I must admit there was a season when my trust was a little off, basically wavering because of what was going on in my life, but I am back now, and I absolutely trust my Heavenly Father.

I don't know if you have had an experience with not trusting, but I hope after reading what follows, your trust level will be increased. When God talks, we listen, enjoy.

Only Believe!

If you just believed in the endless possibilities, you would be a happier person. You would live in a world that seems magical and unreal.

If you believed in the love I have for you, there would never be a time when you would have to beg, plead, borrow, or steal.

If you truly believed in yourself and in the power of who I am, you would declare spectacular moments, years, and a life where people would see your good works and glorify Me, your Heavenly Father (Matthew 5:16).

Life changes when you believe.

If you would only believe, all things would be possible and words like, "can't" and "impossible" would quickly leave your vocabulary (Mark 9:23). The projects that you have put on the shelf to look at later would become works in progress now.

Act!

Imagine what would happen if you allowed your mind to be free from stress, worry, and fear. The thought alone is mind-boggling, is it not? Do you ever think about what your life would look like without those evil triplets? Are you smiling at the very thought? If you are, serve them an eviction notice to leave now, in the name of Jesus.

Now, what do you believe?

If you believed in the power of love, you would not hate nor dislike anyone. In fact, you would quickly forgive every infraction.

If you believed that you assist in making your world what it is, you would work to make it what you want and need it to be.

If you believed you had the power to change the atmosphere in the room, you would shine bright when you entered it.

You can have what you believe.

Believing is essential to living life abundantly. You cannot go around thinking you do not deserve good because you may have done some bad. I love you, and the moment you asked Me to forgive you and meant it, I did and released it (Hebrews 8:12). I am not mad at you; I do not hold grudges and there is no evil in Me. I am love!

My sheep know My voice.

You are My sheep, get to know Me. Some of My ways will rub off on you and before you know it you will learn to love Me. Just as people see similarities in you and your earthly parents, they will begin to see similarities of Me in you. If you believe that I can do anything, and you have accepted Jesus as Lord, what is it that you cannot do?

There is power in My Word.

Greater is He that is within you than he that is in the world (1 John 4:4)! Do you understand that statement and what I have been saying today? You have power! You are walking around weak when you are strong, broke when you can be rich, and for some strange reason, you have chosen sickness instead of health. Just believe!

Believing is everything!

If you want to change your life, believe that you can and do it. Faith is the substance of things hoped for, the evidence of things not seen (Hebrews 11:1). If you want to see what you hope for, you must believe you can have it first. Believing is essential to your life and your relationship with Me.

For a moment, think of something you have that you really wanted. How do you feel about it? Think about your feelings toward it and imagine those feelings being a way of life and not just a momentary emotion. It is possible you know; all things are possible when you believe (Mark 9:23). Will you believe?

What did I say?

Father, I'm listening. You told me to believe in You, in myself, and the life I desire. It is possible to live it. I accept Jesus as Lord and want others to see You in me. I am strong, rich, and healthy, my faith is strengthened through my belief.

Thoughts for you, the Reader...

Life changes when you believe. You can have what you believe. Remember there is power in God's Word. Time for you to reflect...

What stopped you from believing?

_____
_____
_____

How has doubt kept you from experiencing joy?

_____
_____
_____

What will it take for you to believe again?

_____
_____
_____

What Did I Say?

How does believing in God's promises benefit you?

_____
_____
_____
_____

Review the scriptures given for this day and record the God-given revelations.

Hebrews 6:13

_____
_____
_____
_____

Mark 9:23

_____
_____
_____
_____

Matthew 5:16

_____
_____
_____
_____

Hebrews 8:12

1 John 4:4

Hebrews 11:1

When you consider how you believe, what did you hear God say?

Today's Prayer: *Thank You, Father God, for the love You show me with every breath I take. I have allowed unbelief to dominate me in so many areas of life, but no more. I will not doubt. I believe. I know unbelief has kept me from great things and has prolonged my promises. I believe and will continue to do so. Thank You for sharing the possibilities of believing, I am listening to what You say, and I am doing what You tell me to do.*

Today's Affirmations

(Say Aloud)

I am a Believer

I am Full of Income Producing Ideas

I am Capable of. . .(fill in the blank)

Write Your Vision

I decree and declare from this moment forward I will _____

_____
_____
_____
_____
_____
_____
_____
_____
_____
_____

Day 30
Assurance

> "Assurance is firm persuasion; full confidence or trust; freedom from doubt; certain expectation; the utmost certainty."
>
> *(KJV Dictionary)*

God is love. One thing I know for sure is the love of God is real. It is indescribable. I know the Bible says in John 3:16 that God so loved the world that He gave His one and only son, that whoever believes in Him should not perish but have eternal life" (NIV). It says, however, we will never know all Jesus had to endure for us, that's love. There is no love like that, none can come close or compare, for God is love.

On this day, I choose to talk about the goodness of God. In this conversation, He assured me of His love for me. As you read this, my prayer is that something is said that reminds you of the love He has for you.

Love conquers all!

The one thing I am sure of is the love You have for me. At times, the things You allow and the things I do not understand persuade me to doubt Your love, but I never will. Your love makes me smile. Just thinking about how You love me calms my storms and chases away my fears. I am strong in You and feel like I can conquer all. Nothing can bother me when I am basking in Your presence and thinking about Your love. I am secure in You and happy because of You.

I am in awe of You, Lord!

God, I love You! I love the way You love me just as I am. I love how I can be myself with You and not pretend. I love how You are patient with me; it does not bother You if it takes me a day or a year to understand something or someone. Your love is constant, steady, and continuous. What a blessing it is for not only me but for us all!

Assurance

Because of Who You are!

Because of Your Love, I am free. Free to talk to You whenever I want. Free to ask for forgiveness and be assured that I am forgiven. Free to prosper. Free to be healed and delivered from all evil and free to be me. It is not like that with mankind. They want you to be and to act in a way that is pleasing to them. The moment you attempt to be yourself they find fault.

You are a good Father.

You are the perfect father, always coming to the rescue of your children, I love that about You. I love that You care about me in such a deep and intimate way. I never feel like I am asking a stupid question when I talk to You. I feel like a sponge soaking up all types of wisdom, knowledge, and understanding. I feel safe. I feel like I belong and I feel like I matter. In You, Father, I feel very special.

Believe My Words!

You were made in a unique way and everything I created is wonderfully made (Psalm 139:14). Do not alter yourself or your personality for anything or anyone. Forgive people and release every negative word spoken to you that you believed. I am the Master Creator and the way I created you was intentional as is everything I do. Be assured that I make no mistakes and I love you. You do not have to feel insecure about yourself, you were wonderfully made.

Assurance

Thoughts for you, the Reader...

Are you ready to share your feelings?

What are you assured of regarding our Heavenly Father?

_____

_____

_____

_____

How great does it feel expressing yourself in this manner?

_____

_____

_____

_____

Share a situation where you had absolute assurance that God would show up:

_____

_____

_____

_____

Review the scriptures given for this day and record what God reveals to you.

John 3:16

_____

_____

_____

_____

Psalm 139:14

_____

_____

_____

_____

When you consider God's assurance, did you see a connection with His Word?

_____

_____

_____

_____

Assurance

Today's Prayer: *God, You are amazing in every way. The love You have for this world is incredible. The air we breathe, the singing birds, the rays of the sun, I can go on and on about You and the love You have for Your children. Thank You for Your love.*

Today's Affirmations

(Say Aloud)

I am Loved.

I am Unique.

I am Wonderfully Made.

Write Your Vision

I decree and declare from this moment forward I will _____

_____
_____
_____
_____
_____
_____
_____
_____
_____
_____

**GOD LOVES YOU
LIFE IS A JOURNEY;
KEEP YOUR HEAD UP
FINISH STRONG**

Kimberly D. Graham is the author of two previously published books, "Enduring for the Promise" and "The Chosen Generation". She currently lives in GA with her husband and enjoys spending time with her family. Ministry is important and her relationship with God is what matters most. Being a doer of His Word goes far beyond the four walls of any building and she considers it a pleasure that she get to serve.

Get connected: Website - kimberlydgraham.com, @kdginspires on Twitter and Instagram, Facebook – Kimberly D. Graham

CPSIA information can be obtained
at www.ICGtesting.com
Printed in the USA
FSHW021018090819
60861FS